teaching core practices
in teacher education

teaching
core
practices
in teacher
education

edited by

PAM GROSSMAN

Harvard Education Press
Cambridge, Massachusetts

Paperback ISBN 978-1-68253-187-7
Library Edition ISBN 978-1-68253-188-4

Library of Congress Cataloging-in-Publication Data

Names: Grossman, Pamela L. (Pamela Lynn), 1953–
Title: Teaching core practices in teacher education / edited by Pam Grossman.
Description: Cambridge, Massachusetts : Harvard Education Press, 2018. |
    Includes index.
Identifiers: LCCN 2017059545| ISBN 9781682531877 (pbk.) |
    ISBN 9781682531884 (library edition)
Subjects: LCSH: Teacher educators—United States. | Teachers—Training
    of—United States. | Teachers—In-service training—United States. | Teaching.
Classification: LCC LB1715 .T4295 2018 | DDC 370.71/1—dc23
    LC record available at https://lccn.loc.gov/2017059545

Published by Harvard Education Press,
an imprint of the Harvard Education Publishing Group

Harvard Education Press
8 Story Street
Cambridge, MA 02138

Cover Design: Ciano Design
Cover Image: billnoll/E+/Getty Images

The typefaces used in this book are ITC Stone and Museo.

This book is a volume in the Core Practices in Education Series.

*For all of our children, including
my own—Ben, Rebecca, and Sarah—
and for their teachers, who inspired
and challenged them.*

CONTENTS

CHAPTER 1

The Turn Towards Practice in Teacher Education

An Introduction to the Work of the Core Practice Consortium

Pam Grossman, Sarah Schneider Kavanagh,
and Christopher G. Pupik Dean

> I shall assume without argument that adequate professional instruction of teachers is not exclusively theoretical, but involves a certain amount of practical work. The primary question as to the latter is the aim with which it shall be conducted.[1]
>
> —JOHN DEWEY, 1904

To those engaged in contemporary conversations about teacher education, John Dewey's words may seem like they were written yesterday. More than a century has passed since these sentences were penned, and yet the field of teacher education continues to wrestle with the question of how teacher educators should be conducting the practical aspects of preparing teachers for the profession. As the number of teacher educators describing their work as "practice-based" has grown, so has concern in the field that focusing teacher education on practice runs the risk of emphasizing decontextualized skills and routines in ways that erode the agency of the teacher. The work presented in this volume represents the collective efforts of a group of teacher educators that is dedicated to designing approaches to practice-based teacher education that treat

1

the practical work of teaching as work that entails complex thought, professional judgment, and continual reflection. As a collaborative community of teacher educators, we have undertaken this book project to share pedagogical approaches for preparing teachers—approaches that foreground the practical, but see practice as complex, sophisticated, and thoughtful work.

Several years before this book project was imagined, a group of teacher educators, all of whom were experimenting with practice-based approaches to teacher education, convened to discuss their work. This group grew and changed (and continues to grow and change). Because of our shared interest around identifying practices to cultivate in teacher education, the group identified itself as the Core Practice Consortium (CPC). The Consortium began as an effort to bring together scholars and practitioners from different practice-focused groups to collaborate across projects, across grade levels, and across content areas. Our aim was to develop shared understanding and common language concerning what it takes to prepare novice teachers for practice. Ultimately, the Consortium agreed that the group's work would focus on both the core practices of teaching and on the pedagogies of teacher education used to prepare novices to enact those practices in ways that are responsive to the unique needs of their K–12 students. This book project grew out of a desire to share what we have learned through our collaborations and to expand the conversation to include a broader network of teacher educators interested in wrestling with questions about the pedagogies of practice-based teacher education.

Although the authors of this book share a common interest in preparing teachers for practice, we come from varied institutional contexts, differing disciplinary communities, and diverse experiences as teacher educators. Our collaborations have helped us to build bridges of shared language that cross our work. This shared language has supported us in conducting a shared research project and then aggregating knowledge about teaching and the induction of novice teachers and teacher educators into a set of research findings. Our hope now is to extend the conversation to a broader network of teacher educators. If this book can play a part in sparking that conversation, then we have accomplished our goal.

A BRIEF HISTORY OF THE FOCUS ON PRACTICE IN TEACHER EDUCATION

Before focusing on pedagogical approaches to preparing teachers for practice, we believe it is important to reflect on the history of reforms and on current climates in teacher education that have brought us to this focus. A growing body of evidence illustrates the critical role that teaching quality plays in fostering significant and meaningful student learning.[2] At the same time, the ability of teacher education programs to prepare teachers to take on the challenging work of preparing teachers is under scrutiny. University teacher education programs, in particular, have been critiqued for overvaluing knowledge for teaching at the cost of teaching practices and for failing to prepare novices for the complex realities of the classroom.[3] In this atmosphere, the field of teacher education is in the midst of a major shift—a turn away from an intense focus on the knowledge needed for teaching to a focus on the use of that knowledge in practice.[4] The fundamental goal undergirding this turn is to better support teachers in learning how to enact teaching practices skillfully and knowledgeably in ways that support student learning.[5]

This turn to practice, however, is not the first of its kind. All histories are cyclical, and the history of teacher education in the United States is no exception. Reflecting on historical turns to practice in teacher education can support contemporary teacher educators interested in practice-based teacher education and help to avoid the pitfalls of our predecessors. One historical effort to focus on practice was the competency-based teacher education reform movement in the 1960s and 1970s. During this era, competency-based teacher education focused on providing novice teachers with opportunities to practice discrete skills, often divorced from judgment. Resulting teacher evaluation systems featured long checklists of competencies.[6] Reacting to this reductive conception of teaching, reforms in the 1980s focused on teacher thinking, judgment, and knowledge, including subject matter knowledge.[7] Teacher educators began using case-based methods to build teachers' knowledge for making the complex, moment-to-moment decisions required for teaching.[8]

While addressing important aspects of teaching, the focus on knowledge in the 1980s and 1990s failed to support teachers to *use* that knowledge in practice.[9] While teacher candidates had rich opportunities to develop pedagogical thinking, including the ability to reflect on their work, they had fewer opportunities to try out the work of teaching prior to entering the classroom. To address this gap, a number of researchers and teacher educators began to suggest focusing teacher education on core practices for teaching.[10] The concept of core practices was introduced as a way to support teachers and teacher educators to integrate work on developing skills with work on developing the knowledge and judgment required to put those skills to use when working with students.

Practice in complex domains, from a sociocultural perspective, involves the orchestration of understanding, skill, relationship, and identity to accomplish particular activities with others in specific environments.[11] Cultivating practice during professional education thus requires attending to all of these elements. Core practices in teaching are identifiable components (fundamental to teaching and grounded in disciplinary goals) that teachers enact to support learning. Core practices consist of strategies, routines, and moves that can be unpacked and learned by teachers. They are distinct from other efforts to focus on teaching competencies in that core practices are deeply connected to the goals of disciplinary learning and are not simply a checklist of competencies or techniques divorced from principles and theory.[12] Rather, the central goal of the work on core practices is to improve learning opportunities available to all students, and especially those from low-income backgrounds and minority groups.

As interest in identifying foundational practices for teaching has developed, different teacher education programs, research projects, and individual teacher educators have developed their own sets of core practices of teaching. While sets of core practices vary in grain size, content-specificity, exhaustiveness, and other features, most are true to the following characteristics identified by Grossman, Hammerness, and McDonald:

- practices that occur with high frequency in teaching;
- practices that teachers can enact in classrooms across different curricula or instructional approaches;

- practices that allow teachers to learn more about students and about teaching;
- practices that preserve the integrity and complexity of teaching; and
- practices that are research-based and have the potential to improve student achievement.[13]

One of the best known sets of core practices of teaching is TeachingWorks' "high-leverage practices." TeachingWorks' core practices were originally designed to be the organizing framework for the University of Michigan's elementary teacher education program and are specifically focused on novice teachers. Another set of core practices that make up the organizing framework for an entire teacher education program come from the University of Washington's U-ACT program. The grain size of these two sets of practices are very different. While TeachingWorks' practices span a wide variety of teachers' activities (planning, teaching, informal time with students, and communicating with colleagues, families, and community members), the U-ACT core practices only refer to things that teachers do while they are in the midst of instruction. Another way that sets of core practices vary relates to content specificity. While TeachingWorks' practices and U-ACT's practices were designed to cross content areas, other sets of core practices were designed to be content specific. Sets of core practices developed at Stanford University, for example, were created within particular subject matter areas. These include core practices of teaching English language arts, science, and history. (For illustrations of these sets of core teaching practices, please see Appendix.)

While many researchers and teacher educators are working on elements of core practices, we think it is important to highlight the work of a few select groups who have been focused on practice-based teacher education—groups who have been coming together regularly since 2012 to collaborate within the Core Practice Consortium. The sets of core practices that we reference above and include in the appendix of this book come from the work of these groups. We offer brief descriptions of them to provide some examples of practice-focused work in teacher education and to provide some background about the specific research programs that came together to form the CPC.

TeachingWorks and the Teacher Education Initiative at the University of Michigan

Over the past decade, faculty at the University of Michigan have redesigned the curriculum of their elementary teacher education program to be organized around what they called "high-leverage practices" or HLPs. In so doing, the program did away with a program model in which all courses were of equal length and intensity, instead opting for modules of different durations and designs, each tailored to support novice teachers to master particular HLPs. The program included new clinical settings for novices to observe, study, and try out high-leverage practices, and the faculty developed assessments of the HLPs. TeachingWorks grew out of the University of Michigan's program redesign effort, holding the same perspectives on the centrality of practice in learning to teach. However, rather than being internally focused on the University of Michigan, the aim of TeachingWorks was to look beyond the university toward the broader field of teacher education. Key participants in both Teaching-Works and the University of Michigan's teacher education programs have been a part of the CPC since its inception, and their work and ideas have deeply shaped the work we have done together.[14]

Learning In, From, and For Teaching Practice

The Consortium also brought together researchers and teacher educators who had been participating in a research project on practice-based teacher education for teachers of mathematics that spanned multiple universities (including the University of California, Los Angeles; the University of Michigan; and the University of Washington)—the Learning In, From, and For Teaching Practice or the LTP project. Through this project, math education researchers developed shared "instructional activities" through which they taught novice teachers about mathematics, students' mathematical thinking, and teaching practices. Along with the instructional activities, the group also developed a design for teacher preparation organized around cycles of enactment and investigation. This includes a signature pedagogical approach to working with novice teachers that involves public rehearsals of practice. Like the consortium participants from the University of Michigan, the researchers involved in the LTP project developed shared ways of thinking and talking about practice-based teacher education that became central to the collective work of the broader consortium.[15]

Stanford University's Center to Support Excellence in Teaching (CSET)

The first meeting of what was to become the CPC was hosted by Stanford University's Center to Support Excellence in Teaching. Participants from this community brought their experience conducting studies of both core practices of teaching[16] and of pedagogical approaches used by professional educators to prepare novices for professional practice.[17] Researchers at CSET developed lists of core teaching practices specific to particular content areas, some as part of a research study on the teaching of English language arts,[18] and others from Delphi studies, which involved convening panels of education researchers, teacher educators, teachers, and scholars in the disciplines.[19] CSET researchers also used these practices, along with their earlier research on the pedagogy of professional practice, as the curricular groundwork for the design of the Hollyhock Fellowship program, a practice-focused professional development program for early-career teachers.

The University of Washington's Ambitious Science Teaching Project

Also represented in the consortium were researchers from the University of Washington who had been studying core practices of ambitious science teaching. These researchers and teacher educators developed a set of core practices of science teaching and began conducting research on whether and in what ways novice teachers who had been prepared to teach these practices were bringing these practices into their work with K–12 students. This group was focused specifically on the role that tools played in supporting teachers to adopt and integrate new practices into their teaching.[20]

While each of these groups of researchers had a distinct focus to their work, all were engaged in work that wrestled with how best to support novice teachers in developing more ambitious teaching through focusing on a set of practices or instructional activities. The CPC began as a way to support representatives of these groups to share their work and use each others' expertise to develop a more common understanding of these practice-based approaches to supporting novice teachers. Our work began with an effort to define a common understanding of what we mean by core practice and then to unpack a few specific core practices in some depth by identifying and describing their components. Readers can find the CPC's initial definition of the term "core practice" and of facilitating discussion as a core practice in the Appendix. That section also includes the specifications for facilitating classroom discussion that were developed by the English language arts and Science teams. Over time, new members have joined the Consortium who were not affiliated with these early projects, new projects have developed out of the collaborations formed within the Consortium, and a significant amount of research has been produced on practice-based approaches to teacher education.[21] This book is our attempt at synthesizing what we have learned about pedagogical approaches to practice-based teacher education through these collaborations.

PEDAGOGIES OF TEACHER EDUCATION

Emerging from their study of professional education for practitioners engaged in relational practices, such as teaching, ministry, and clinical psychology, Grossman and her colleagues have developed a framework for the teaching of practice that included the elements of representation of practice, decomposition of practice, and approximation of practice.[22] This framework tries to account for the underlying structure of different pedagogies used in professional education, particularly pedagogies that are deeply grounded in practice. Representations of practice include all of the different ways in which the work of practitioners is made visible to novices during professional education. Such representations include everything from the stories told by practitioners about practice, to written narratives and case studies, to videos of actual practice. Representations can also include artifacts from practice, including lesson plans, student work, and live observations of practitioners or forms of instructional rounds. Much of professional education involves learning from different representations of practice, including the modeling of practice by teacher educators. With the increasing availability of video recordings of class-room teaching, the use of video representations has become a staple of teacher education. In this volume, we explore what it means to use both modeling and video representations of teaching to introduce novices to the practice of facilitating discussion.

Part of the challenge of learning from representations of practice is knowing how to look, what to look for, and how to interpret what is ob-served.[23] For this reason, part of the pedagogy of using representations of practice involves the "decomposition" of practice—breaking down a com-plex practice into its constituent parts for the purposes of teaching and learning.[24] In making facets of practice visible to novices, decompositions of practice in professional education can help develop professional vi-sion.[25] At the same time, these decompositions also help support students as they learn to enact complex practices. By focusing on one component of a more complex practice, such as following up on student ideas in a discussion, for example, novices have opportunities to develop fluency in a more discrete set of moves or strategies.

The ability to decompose practice depends upon the existence of a language and structure for describing practice—what we've described as a grammar of practice. Without such a grammar, it is difficult to name the parts or to know how the components are related to one another. Part of the effort to delineate core or high-leverage practices for teachers is to build such a language for describing practice.

Approximations of practice provide novices with the opportunity to enact elements of practice with a high degree of support and under condi-tions of reduced complexity. Virtually all professional education includes opportunities for students to engage in approximations of practice. In activities ranging from role-plays to moot court and student teaching, approximations require students to engage in practice that is related, but not identical, to the work of practicing professionals. Approximations can also provide opportunities for novices to engage in "deliberate practice"[26] of particularly challenging components of practice.

Because they can often be paused midstream, pedagogies that use approximations of practice also provide the opportunity for specific and targeted feedback. In this volume, we'll explore the use of a range of approximations, including rehearsals, for helping teacher candidates learn to facilitate discussion.

THE CORE PRACTICE CONSORTIUM: CORE PRACTICES AND THE PEDAGOGIES OF TEACHER EDUCATION

Drawing on the knowledge gained through reflection on past reform efforts, and in keeping with Lortie's charge to work toward a "common technical vocabulary,"[27] the Core Practice Consortium came together around a shared commitment to a focus on practice and a belief that the work of building the field of teacher education around this focus requires greater understanding among those who are doing the work. At our very first meeting, we grappled with the different terms we used to describe our work—from core practices to high-leverage practices to instructional activity—and tried to find common ground. From this foundation, the group has built a collaborative research agenda that supports a variety of work and collaborations for five years and counting. The primary research project involved teacher educators from ten institutional contexts studying how they taught novice teachers the core practice of discussion. Through these years of engagement, the group developed and refined a theory of action for building the field of teacher education and practices and principles that supported this theory of action. We want to share this theory of action and the supporting practices in the hopes that readers of this volume might better understand the conditions that supported the learning we share in this volume. We also hope that the CPC might serve as an example to others who wish to adopt similar collaborative structures to support the development of their own professional communities of teacher educators. We have found that these structures have supported our own learning and we hope that others might find them useful as well.

Over the years, the focus on Lortie's "common technical vocabulary" has evolved into an understanding that building the field of teacher education requires the construction of a professional community of teacher educators who are working toward common understandings, language, and practice. There are certainly many ways that teacher educators are already working toward this goal, but the CPC set out to build this community in novel ways. A primary strategy was, and remains, setting up situations where teacher educators must work across different contexts. The CPC has supported teacher educators to bridge three primary contexts that typically remain isolated in teacher education: institutions, subject areas, and grade levels. The research teams in the CPC are composed of researchers from different institutions and who focus their research on different grade levels. In their work, these teams must develop common understandings around practice and teacher education pedagogy in order to effectively carry out their research programs. For example, a team of English language arts (ELA) teacher educators had to develop a common understanding of the practice of discussion when, based on grade-level contexts, they had vastly different conceptions of what constitutes a discussion. The elementary teacher educators saw discussion as something that could occur within a few minutes, but secondary teacher educators saw a discussion as occurring over an extended period of time. While the teams themselves are organized around subject matter expertise, consortium-wide conversations and research efforts require engagement and common understanding across these contexts as well.

The team structures of the CPC provided teacher educators with the opportunity to interact, but these interactions could not be generative, nor support the development of common understanding and shared language, if they did not challenge participants to do real work together. In other words, the work of the teams had to require them to move past a simple acknowledgement of different perspectives that are driven by contextual differences. Instead, it had to demand that they find a resolution to these differences. Since the CPC was composed primarily of researchers, the driving motivation for this group became the production of research concerning the core practices of teaching and the pedagogies of teacher education. Achieving this goal required the development of more than surface-level understandings in order to develop shared tools and resources.

One of the primary tools used to develop this shared understanding in the earlier portions of the CPC's work was the process of creating specifications of core practice and pedagogies of teacher education.

Developing specifications for the pedagogies and practices required sub-ject matter teams (composed of researchers from different institutional and grade-level contexts) to define the pedagogy or practice, list its com-ponents, and provide examples of its use in action. The teams then pre-sented these specifications to the larger CPC group. The groups and the CPC as a whole had to come to a high level of agreement in order to move forward with the research process. Reaching this agreement necessitated the development of shared understanding around the practice of facili-tating discussion. Even if each member of the team did not completely agree with the final specification, they had to have an understanding of the positions of the other team members in order to consent to the spec-ification on offer.

Later in the research process, once the teacher educators were con-ducting research on their efforts to teach novice teachers the core prac-tice of discussion, other structures supported the development of shared understanding. One of these was opening up teacher educators' practice to other teacher educators. In the project, members of the CPC were the primary research subjects and recorded, shared, and collaboratively ana-lyzed their own practice as teacher educators. Some veteran teacher edu-cators admitted that this was the first time that another teacher educator had observed their practice. This exposure provided the opportunity for members of the CPC to ask questions and engage in conversations based on actual observations and video clips of teacher education rather than through recollections shared in discussion.

The CPC is now a collaboration of teacher educators from eleven teacher education programs across the United States. Part of our hope was to test the approach to teacher education pedagogy we have developed across a wide variety of contexts. The programs include both university-based and non-university-based programs and undergraduate and gradu-ate programs; the programs also vary in terms of their curricula, overall structure, and field experiences. The consortium's work creates a space for focused ongoing learning within teacher education, where teacher edu-cators can work toward shared language and understandings of the core practices of teaching and pedagogies of teacher education through collab-orative construction of artifacts, tools, and research efforts. In this effort, the CPC attends to issues of equity in education by building a vision of teaching that takes students' emotional, social, and intellectual resources seriously in disciplinary learning. The CPC takes the view that teachers' actions are consequential for countering longstanding inequities in the schooling experiences of children, particularly youth from marginalized communities. An emphasis on core practices does not preclude a critical examination of the structures that have shaped schooling in the US or the deeply relational and contextualized ways that teachers make decisions and support children's learning.

OVERVIEW OF THE VOLUME

In the following chapters of the book, we describe a variety of pedagogies of teacher education, focusing on the uses of various representations and approximations of practice. In chapter 2, the authors explore the use of representations in teacher education and outline principles for selecting the type of representation that will be used and the principles for using specific representations. The chapter will then discuss the ways representations are used in teacher education, highlighting the different types of representations and providing examples in the form of vignettes.

In chapter 3, the authors dive more deeply into the use of modeling in teacher education. Modeling allows a teacher educator to reveal why an expert teacher might call on one student over another, why a teacher might rephrase a student's comment and ask another student to offer a counterargument, or why a teacher might pause the discussion to review critical content. In addition to presenting a rationale for and description of modeling as a pedagogy for teaching core practices in teacher education, the authors provide several examples of modeling in methods courses, closing with a discussion of the challenges to using modeling effectively and with suggestions for how teacher educators might navigate these challenges.

Chapter 4 addresses the use of approximations in teacher education to support the development of practice. The chapter outlines critical features of approximations and shares vignettes of teacher educators using a range of approximations in different contexts and disciplines. It also sets out some principles of selection for identifying and using approximations in teacher education across different subject matters. Each vignette is accompanied by affordances and constraints of specific approximations, as well as recommendations for implementation.

Chapter 5 provides a deep dive into the pedagogy of rehearsals as an example of a generative approximation of practice. The authors discuss the roles of the teacher educator, the roles of the preservice teachers, and the nature of interactions that happen between them in rehearsal. The chapter illustrates how teacher educators use rehearsals to deepen novice teachers' content knowledge and to support their understanding of student thinking and ways to respond to it.

In Chapter 6, the authors provide a broad overview of how core practices fit into the teacher education curriculum. They argue that core practices and teacher educator pedagogies serve as tools for teacher educators to support teacher candidates in learning how to enact practices in relation to a set of theories, principles, goals and commitments within a teacher education program. The teacher education program, the conceptualization of the domain, the theories drawn upon to guide learning, and the structures of the methods courses all shape the use of teacher educator pedagogies and core practices. The chapter provides a set of vignettes to illustrate how local contexts, including programmatic structures and commitments, shape the pedagogies designed to cultivate core practices.

Chapter 7 illustrates how these pedagogies can be used beyond preservice teacher education to support practicing teachers. The authors argue that for core practice work to succeed, it needs to be responsive to the demands and realities of bringing this work to school settings, and the chapter provides examples of how these pedagogies can be used in the context of field settings and professional development.

We conclude this volume with a coda that includes a series of vignettes that illustrate how we have used our work on practice to build bridges across the fissures that have for too long fragmented our work, and we offer to the field images of a more collaborative future. The work of the Consortium began with conversation and continued with collaboration. It is our hope that this book will open that conversation to a wider group of teacher educators who are interested in practice-based approaches to teacher education and provide more opportunities for continued collaboration.

CHAPTER 2

Use of Representations in Teacher Education

Katie A. Danielson, Meghan Shaughnessy, and Lightning Peter Jay

This chapter addresses the use of representations of practice in teacher education. Representations "comprise the different ways that practice is represented in professional education and what these various representations make visible to novices."[1] Teacher educators provide representations such as video records, student work, or lesson plans to teacher candidates (henceforth TCs) both to support the candidates in seeing practice as a whole and also to allow them to dive into particular components of a lesson. Representations provide a common moment of teaching to discuss and unpack. This chapter outlines principles for selecting the type of representation to use and provides characteristics of the specific representations. The chapter then discusses the ways representations are used in teacher education, highlighting the different types of representations and providing examples in the form of vignettes. The chapter ends with a consideration of what facets of practice are made visible or hidden in different types of representations.

Representations of practice are used across professional education. In medical school, students spend their third year observing doctors across specialties. These multiple observations make different aspects of the daily work of various specialties visible to medical students. Law students watch videos of oral arguments as a representation of litigation, demonstrating how legal writing is used in a court room. Examples of representations used in teacher education include videos, teacher educator modeling, case studies, planning templates, classroom transcripts, and classroom observations.

In addition to providing examples of teaching practice, representations allow the decomposition of practice—an unpacking of complex practice—for professionals in their preparation. In law school, for example, students will often watch a clip of just the closing arguments of a trial. The final argument a lawyer makes before the jury deliberates is a critical moment in a legal case. Therefore, it is an important component for law students to focus in on and examine carefully. Showing just one part of the trial creates a space for candidates to dive into the specific argument and language that one might use in a part of the whole.

Representations may also be used as a springboard for an approximation of practice. For example, in problem-based medical education, medical students may read a case about a patient (a representation of practice). Individually, the medical students will then enter a room where they will need to interact with an actor taking on the role of the patient in an approximation of a medical exam. The patient case read by the medical students serves as a representation of the medical chart that doctors often read prior to seeing a patient for the first time.

In selecting or developing representations of practice, it is important to consider the facets of practice that are or are not made visible by the representation.[2] For example, a video of classroom teaching can make visible how children respond to questions that a teacher poses in a lesson. In contrast, the children's thinking, including their responses, would not be authentically represented in a representation consisting of a teacher educator modeling a core practice with a group of TCs. Careful consideration of representations requires a teacher educator to have a sense of the teaching practices and content they want to make visible to the candidates.

In addition to selecting a representation, it is important to consider the activities that will take place before and after the representations are presented. How will the representation be introduced? What preparatory work may need to be done around the K–12 content in the representation? How will the teacher educator unpack the representation? Will there first be a discussion, or will the representation launch into an approximation? As teacher educators, it is essential to consider the work that will occur around the representation with as much purpose as the selection of the representation itself.

EXAMPLES OF REPRESENTATIONS OF PRACTICE
IN TEACHER EDUCATION

We next turn to examples of the use of representations in teacher education courses across three different content areas and contexts. These examples are: (1) using a planning template and lesson plan; (2) using transcripts of classroom talk; and (3) linking a video representation with an approximation. For each example, we describe the teacher educator's reasoning behind selecting a particular type of representation, as well as the particulars of the representation that was selected. The examples illustrate the ways in which the representations served as a means to support TCs in learning to teach. We also acknowledge the limitations of the representations that were used.

Example 1: Using Multiple Representations
of Practice in Elementary Literacy

The first example comes from the University of Washington's Accelerated Certification for Teachers program (U-ACT). The program is designed around principles and core practices, and engages teachers in a learning cycle that includes the introduction of content, preparation, enactment, and analysis.[3] In this example, the literacy teacher educator, Katie Danielson, is teaching candidates about a specific instructional activity,[4] an interactive read-aloud, in which a teacher facilitates a group of children in a focused discussion around a text. The discussion engages the students in wrestling with the content of the text and using reading strategies. But teaching novice teachers to engage in this instructional activity is not trivial, and in her class, Katie encountered a problem which led her to design specific representations of practice to use with her TCs.

Katie had previously provided candidates with three representations of the instructional activity. The first was a teacher educator model of an interactive read-aloud with the text *Yesterday I Had the Blues*.[5] Then, candidates watched a video of the same lesson being taught to a class of kindergarten children. Katie intentionally aligned the representations to be around the same text because she wanted TCs to be familiar with the content of the story and the focal reading strategy so they could focus on elements of the read-aloud. The first two representations included actual lessons, so for the third, Katie sought to provide candidates with a representation that took out the complexities that occur when a lesson is taught, encouraging candidates to focus on the components of the lesson. Therefore, the third representation was an interactive read-aloud instructional activity planning template.[6] In this template, an interactive read-aloud is broken down into four components: transitioning into the lesson, and sections for before, during, and after reading.

Katie selected the planning template representation because she wanted to make visible some of the thinking behind the lessons the TCs had previously seen. While the teacher educator model provided a space for candidates to discuss why particular moves were made, it did not provide documentation of that thinking for candidates to refer to later on in the course. The questions included in the template are not just about the specific lesson, but are designed to help candidates transfer knowledge from specific examples to the general considerations needed when planning any interactive read-aloud. Additionally, Katie wanted to highlight the different components of the lesson and the subcomponents within each part. For example, the "before reading" component (figure 2.1), which is crucial for providing children with access to the content and setting them up for

FIGURE 2.1 *Interactive read-aloud instructional activity template: Before Reading section*

STEP 3: BEFORE READING:	
• Activate background knowledge or prior learning and connect it to the text or today's lesson.	
• Frame the text for students. Think about: how will you scaffold the introduction of the text to provide all students with access?	
• Name the reading strategy you will be working on and how it helps readers (process objective).	
• Set the purpose for reading.	

(1) model for them
(2) video of children
(3) lesson plan → scaffolding prior knowledge
(4) scripted lesson plan, if needed

reading the text, has four critical steps that candidates might not have noticed as they watched the model or video lesson. The template decomposes "before reading" into these four subcomponents. While the candidates had seen these subcomponents included in earlier representations of the lesson, the template explicitly sets out each subcomponent for the candidates, providing reminders of the elements and posing questions for candidates to think about when developing their own plan.

Candidates used the template provided as the third representation to develop their first interactive read-aloud plans. Katie provided individual feedback to candidates prior to their enactment. In addition to helping candidates create strong plans for their first interactive read-aloud, the lesson plan review served as a formative assessment on how well candidates understood the K–12 content and the practices bounded inside the instructional activity. Katie noticed that she was consistently providing candidates with the same feedback. She was providing the language for candidates to use when introducing the focal reading strategy of the lesson, and she was adding or deleting questions that did not connect to the content objective of the texts. While candidates appeared to understand the components of the lesson and the questions to consider when planning, they were experiencing challenges in aligning their lesson to objectives and in using child-friendly language more likely to provide children with access to the text and content.

Reflecting on candidate lesson plans, Katie realized the need for a representation that both decomposed an interactive read-aloud to a finer grain and included specific examples. Katie created a fourth representation to give to candidates, a scripted lesson plan for the interactive read-aloud. Along with the interactive read-aloud instructional activity planning template, Katie included the lesson plan that candidates had experienced as students during the teacher educator modeling and seen in the video representation.

The lesson was specifically written for novices. Because candidates had heard the text multiple times, they were familiar with the content. Additionally, the lesson was focused on making inferences, a strategy that had been central to previous class activities. This allowed the candidates to focus in on other aspects of the lesson rather than on the complexities of a new reading strategy. With her specific TCs in mind, Katie incorporated the language she had previously modeled in the course into the plan and then talked with candidates about how they would need to think about modifications for the specific children in their classrooms, such as how candidates might connect the lesson to prior learning. Having spent time in her candidates' classrooms, Katie knew that many TCs were still learning to incorporate think-time for students into their facilitation of discussions. During many of her observations, she would hold her hands up in the back to help candidates count to ten after asking a question and before having children share or turn-and-talk to their partners. Therefore, Katie included "count to ten" in parentheses in the lesson plan document after a question was posed. Katie found that the written plan not only served as a representation of what a teacher would say during the lesson but that she could also incorporate some of the in-the-moment teacher thinking as an additional support.

Figure 2.2 shows the "before reading" component of the revised third and fourth representations. Together, these representations provide the components of the interactive read-aloud instructional activity and a scripted lesson plan for the text *Yesterday I Had the Blues*.[7] The lesson plan makes visible specific child-friendly language that is likely to give children access to the text and reading strategy. The representations make visible the importance of clearly stating the reading strategy, and they provide developmentally appropriate language to introduce the strategy to a group of kindergarten children. Candidates can see from the plan how the same or similar language is used multiple times within a component of the lesson. While all learners engage in the process of making inferences, it can be difficult to explain, especially to a group of five year olds, what "making an inference" means. The specific language in the plan represents a type of specialized content knowledge for teaching reading.[8]

It is important to keep in mind the full suite of representations to be used along with other pedagogies in the course. Katie's example demonstrates how the alignment among the four representations balances facets of practice that are and are not made visible in each one, and it shows how a fuller understanding of the elements of practice can be developed across multiple representations.[9]

FIGURE 2.2 *Yesterday I Had the Blues lesson plan: Before Reading component*

STEP 3: BEFORE READING:	
• Activate background knowledge or prior learning and connect it to the text or today's lesson. • Frame the text for students. Think about: how will you scaffold the introduction of the text to provide all students with access? • Name the reading strategy you will be working on and how it helps readers (process objective). • Set the purpose for reading.	*Have you ever had a day where you just felt sad? Maybe everything seemed to go wrong? You woke up late and ran out the door without your backpack, or someone wasn't very nice to you on the playground? Show a quiet thumb up if you have had a day where you felt sad.* Give students think time. (Count to ten in your head.) *On days like that, sometimes it's really hard for us to describe how we're feeling. Some people might describe that unhappy, sad feeling by saying they have the blues. Maybe you've heard that before, I've got the blues.* *Today we're going to read a story about a really creative boy who thinks about the world in a colorful way. He uses colors to describe people's feelings. The story about this character is called Yesterday I Had the Blues.* Show students the cover of the book when introducing the title. Point to the boy when talking about the boy. *I've got the blues. Think about what that means, and show me a face of someone who has the blues.* *You're going to see that "blue" is not the only color this boy uses to describe feelings. As we read, look very closely at the pictures because they'll help us understand how and why the characters feel the way they do.*

Source: Kristine M. Schutz and Katie A. Danielson, "Interactive Read Aloud Plan: *Yesterday I Had the Blues*" (unpublished document, University of Washington, 2014).

Example 2: Using Transcripts as a Representation of Practice in a Social Studies Methods Class

As part of the University of Pennsylvania's Teacher Education Program, Abby Reisman teaches Social Studies Methods for secondary teacher candidates. Both the general program and Abby's course marry disciplinary concepts to classroom instructional practices to give candidates a basis for both immediate and long-term success.

One classroom practice emphasized throughout the course is facilitation of historical discussions. Discussions can be intimidating for TCs who must learn to prime a class with background information, pose disciplinarily grounded central questions, set ground rules for engagement, and balance student contributions with the need to steer the conversation. Accordingly, Abby's course provides repeated exposure to a variety of representations of this thorny practice. At the outset of the semester, Abby provided a representation of this practice through modeling a discussion; TCs participated as students in a discussion facilitated by Abby, who helped them in unpacking both their experience and some of her choices and moves. Candidates also watched multiple videos of both expert and developing facilitators and reflected on videos of their own facilitation. Video representations can help candidates understand both the components and gestalt of historical discussions, but the rapid pace of discussions and the kinetic environment of a classroom provide persistent distractions. For novices learning to scan a classroom, listen to students, and react appropriately, it is often difficult to isolate and focus on what the teachers and students are saying. Abby found that candidates consistently focused on the number of hands raised or the tone of the participants instead of evaluating the actual words being said. She began to rethink the representations of practice she was using, considering representations that might make the content of the discussion more visible while making other elements of teaching, such as management, less prominent. Abby decided to turn to transcripts.

Abby wanted to show her candidates that what makes an academic conversation most meaningful is the quality of student comments. Abby also wanted candidates to be aware that there are different ways in which discussions may be facilitated. Aiming to set a meaningful floor for discussion, Abby used transcripts from a prior research study.[10] She selected transcripts where student comments were clearly driven by teacher questions and connected to primary source documents. This meant that candidates would be comparing two discussions that were at least partially successful. Abby wanted to focus candidates' attention on how student comments differentiate good discussions from great ones. Therefore, Abby selected two transcripts of authentic and successful classrooms with students that candidates could compare. The two representations Abby selected were transcripts of classroom discussions about American motivations for entering World War I. Both transcripts come from experienced eleventh-grade US History teachers trained to use a Document-Based Lesson structure in San Francisco public schools. Each transcript runs two pages, records the teacher and multiple students, and takes under five minutes to read. In the first transcript, the teacher, Lisa, uses the documents as a launching point:

> **T:** S1, according to Wilson, why did the U.S. enter WWI?
>
> **S1:** He believed that the German government would be at war with the government and people of the U.S.
>
> **T:** Okay, why did he believe that? What was happening? (big pause) I mean Germany was at war, I mean, but what specifically was happening?
>
> **S1:** American ships were sinking.
>
> **T:** Okay, so we have American ships sinking. Anything else?
>
> **S1:** Democracy.
>
> **T:** Okay, fighting for democracy. Democracy, freedom. Anything else?
>
> **S2:** The right to govern their own people.

After this grounding in the text, Lisa heightens the emotional impact of America's entry into the war by connecting it to the relatable imagery of a schoolyard fight.

> **S5:** I think if you—if we was fighting with Germany or whatever country was trading with Germany, they could've came and tried to have war with us cause you know . . . I don't know . . . (T laughs.) . . . I'm just saying though, why even just . . . I don't know. I just think that's getting into other people's business. So what? They bombed our ships—what else do we got? We got plenty more! (T laughs.) That's an excuse.
>
> **T:** So if someone comes and hits you, you're just going to be like, "whatever?"

S5: I'm going to be like, "you hit me, I'm suing you!" (T laughs hard.) Simple as that . . .

T: You're not going to hit 'em back, S5?

S5: No! (squeal of protest)

Ss: That's a lie! That's a lie! (Lot of laughter; T laughs hard.)

The second teacher, Melanie, begins by soliciting student opinions before diving into the text.

T: So this table, according to the textbook and Wilson, what do you think about the reasons the U.S. went to war? Sshh. Let's listen to this table. Did you think they should have entered WWI?

S1: I said "yes" because um, like, Germany sunk American ships and Germany was trying to interrupt U.S. trade and it was true that they were disrupting (inaudible) . . .

T: Okay. So, S1 gave several reasons she got from the textbook, and that part about democracy that sounds like it comes from Wilson.

S1: Yeah.

T: And so she would argue "yes" based on those two things, the U.S. should have entered. Anything anyone else over here wants to add—S2?

At the end of the transcript, Melanie and her students are still pivoting between text and student opinion.

T: Well, he's making a point, according to the book they were blowing up ships and who was dying?

Ss: Americans.

T: Americans, so President Wilson, if you were the president and somebody was blowing up your people, right?

S4: You blow 'em up.

T: What about the back table, what do you guys think?

S6: Uh. I think we should have gone into war because you read all about neutrality and then he says neutrality is no longer feasible because they're blowing up our ships, so . . .

T: Okay so again we're seeing this idea of revenge. Just a show of hands, how many of you wrote that "yes, the U.S. should have gone to war based on those things?" (half raise hands)

After candidates read through both transcripts Abby asked candidates for their initial reactions to the transcripts. The majority of the candidates said they preferred Lisa's discussion facilitation. Citing her evident rapport with students and the high levels of student engagement, candidates quickly pointed out some of Lisa's best qualities as a teacher. In contrast, they said that Melanie's students seemed slower to participate and their discussion lacked the zest of the discussion in Lisa's class. In fact, Melanie's discussion ended in the same way it began, by polling students. Some candidates saw this as evidence that the discussion failed to make ground. Having purposefully selected these contrasting transcripts, Abby directed the candidates' attention to the content of student comments, shifting the consensus.

Rather than seeing Melanie's transcript as a failure to launch, TCs realized that between the two instances of polling the room Melanie teased out greater depth and wider participation. A closer reading of Lisa's transcript reveals that the shift from a text-based conversation to one based on schoolyard politics is largely driven by a single student who dominates the midsection of the transcript. The ending, quoted above, shows a student attempting to return to the initial historical discussion, but being distracted by the analogy. Abby intentionally neither villainizes nor lionizes Lisa and Melanie, but by the end of the class most candidates are excited about the merits of Melanie's discussion. Having guided candidates to that conclusion, Abby's last move as a facilitator was metacognitive. She reflected on how candidates' internal rubric for discussion was affected by careful reading of student comments, and challenged candidates to listen with the same care they use to read.

Affordances and Constraints of the Transcripts as Representations   The use of transcripts as a representation of practice, while less common than video, can help focus candidates' attention on specific student answers and teacher statements. Abby's use of transcripts also allowed candidates to review each classroom discussion several times. It is time-consuming to replay a video several times, but candidates can move throughout the transcript unimpeded. Transcripts are also easier to edit. Although Abby, in this instance, chose to present real transcripts, there may be occasions where a teacher educator wants a cleaner exemplar and would choose to excerpt or even revise parts of the transcript for pedagogical purposes. Transcripts of course have limitations. They can be time-consuming to prepare, and their limited frame can obscure important pieces of information about students' tone, body language, and classroom context. However, as this example illustrates, despite these limitations, Abby's use of transcripts made visible elements of practice that were less prominent in previous representations. As was true in the earlier example, part of the role of teacher educators is to think about how different types of representations can be used to focus TCs' attention on different elements of practice.

Example 3: Linking Video Representations with Approximations in Elementary Mathematics

Meghan Shaughnessy teaches an elementary mathematics methods course in the undergraduate elementary teacher education program at the University of Michigan. Learning to lead mathematics discussions is a focus of the course, and TCs are supported to engage in this work through a variety of different activities, including enacting discussions with children. A recurrent challenge is helping candidates learn how to conclude discussions in ways that are responsive to the ideas that are shared in the discussion, linked to future learning opportunities for the specific students in the discussion, and aimed at disrupting existing social hierarchies in the classroom.

In past iterations of the course, Meghan showed a video of a mathematics discussion, with a particular focus on the conclusion to the discussion, as a representation of practice. Then, she facilitated conversation with TCs focused on the conclusion. Candidates worked in small groups to draft possible conclusions to a discussion that they were going to facilitate in their field placement classrooms. But this use of video had limitations. It did not provide teacher candidates with opportunities to *practice* the work of teaching. Additionally, the conclusions that candidates gave in their field placement after engaging in the video analysis often seemed pre-scripted; they were not responsive to the ideas that had been shared in the discussion. Along with colleagues in the Mathematics Methods Planning Group at the University of Michigan, Meghan redesigned the activity to use a representation of practice, a video, as a springboard for an approximation of practice, practice in concluding a discussion.

A Description of the Activity   The activity involves three parts. First, TCs engage with the mathematics task that will be focal in the video and anticipate different ways that children might approach and solve the mathematics task. Second, TCs view a mathematics discussion, and the video is paused before the teacher concludes the discussion. Third, the TCs work in small groups to try out concluding the discussion with particular purposes in mind (for example, wrapping up the discussion for the day in a way that allows the class to return to the discussion on another day or highlighting a particularly productive pattern of student thinking). TCs take turns taking on the role of the teacher and concluding the discussion, while their peers observe and give feedback. Before describing each part of the activity in more depth, we turn to the selection of the representation of practice for this discussion.

Selecting the Video   When selecting the video for the activity, Meghan deliberately looked for a mathematics discussion with several different features. First, she wanted a video that would allow for teachers to have different purposes in mind as they concluded the discussion. She wanted TCs to gain exposure to different types of conclusions, and she knew that because time in the course was limited, it was unlikely that she would be able to carry out this same activity multiple times with different videos, so she needed a video that would allow TCs to explore concluding with several different purposes in mind. In this particular case, she selected a video in which fifth grade students were engaged in a discussion of naming a fractional point on a number line. During the discussion, three different names for the point were shared, and the focus was on understanding the different approaches that had been taken by children to name the point.

There was no consensus about the answer at the point that the teacher wrapped up the discussion.

Second, she was looking for mathematics content which was well-matched with mathematical topics that TCs had had opportunities to investigate in the teacher education program. She selected fractions because the topic was the primary focus in a prior methods course, and because she believed that TCs were well-positioned to think about a mathematics discussion about fractions content, and she wanted TCs to see children having discussions about "hard" mathematics topics.

Third, although the orchestration of the discussion was not the primary focus of the activity, she looked for a video that contained a strong representation of the practice of discussion. In other words, she wanted an example of a discussion in which the class was collectively building knowledge through considering and engaging with others' ideas. This is because Meghan sought to give TCs additional exposure to examples in which teachers and students were engaged in rich discussions where the teacher and students were leveraging the resources of students in the classrooms.

Engaging with the Mathematics   Meghan designed the activity so that TCs would first engage in the ~~mathematics of the~~ task themselves. This had two components. First, she had TCs solve the task represented in figure 2.3 themselves so that they would be oriented to the mathematics that children would be discussing in the video. It would be important that candidates were on the same page with the answer to the question ($\frac{1}{3}$, or its mathematical equivalent). Second, she had TCs anticipate the incorrect answers that children might produce along with the reasoning that they might use. For example, some students might name the point $\frac{1}{6}$ because it is $\frac{1}{6}$ of the distance on the line, which does not take into account that the unit on the number line is the interval from 0 to 1, or its equivalent. Meghan facilitated conversation around these patterns of student thinking after TCs had had time to engage with the task. Importantly, she sought to help TCs identify what particular incorrect answers would suggest about students' understandings and how these understandings might be leveraged in instruction. This part of the activity served as an opportunity to deepen TCs' mathematical knowledge for teaching.[11]

FIGURE 2.3 *A fifth-grade number line task*

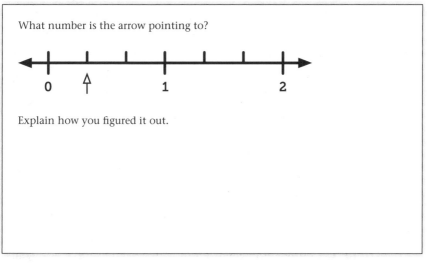

What number is the arrow pointing to?

0   1   2

Explain how you figured it out.

Viewing the Mathematics Discussion   Meghan had TCs view the video which intentionally stopped right before the discussion is concluded. She had candidates keep track of the different ideas that were shared by students as well as the productive ways in which individuals and the collective were engaging in discussion together. The viewing focus was important; the goal was not to track the teacher's moves, rather the goal was to listen carefully to what the children were saying (and not saying) and how they were engaging in the discussion. These observations would be crucial for concluding the discussion. TCs were aware that they would be practicing concluding the discussion.

Concluding the Discussion   Shifting from a representation of practice to an opportunity to enact practice, the next stage of the activity entailed having TCs practice concluding the activity in groups of four or five. Each group was assigned one of three purposes for their concluding discussion: (1) highlight student thinking or responses that were notable in some way; (2) connect the discussion to past mathematical work; and (3) reinforce productive discussion norms. Each group was provided with additional supports related to their purpose. For example, the "reinforcing productive discussion norms" group was given two possible techniques to consider: highlighting a productive thought process or way of working (e.g., listening to other student's ideas), or reflecting on what students have accomplished in the lesson in terms of maintaining productive norms. Because Meghan wanted TCs to practice using specifics from the discussion in their conclusion, she also provided them with a transcript of the discussion (another representation of practice, as discussed in the history methods course example).

Once each group had their purpose, their task was to discuss together how to use one of the given techniques to conclude the discussion with the given purpose in mind. Once they had an initial conversation, TCs in the group took turns carrying out the conclusion in front of their peers. This last piece is crucial, as it requires TCs to practice the work of teaching. As groups engaged in the activity, Meghan circulated and posed questions for the groups to consider as they tried out their conclusions. For example, she noticed that a TC was making a statement about students listening well during a discussion, but the candidate did not signal anything specific that students were doing, such as using another student's idea and referencing that individual, or asking a question about an idea that has been shared. In response, Meghan suggested that the candidate ground that statement in a specific instance that occurred in the discussion.

Importantly, TCs were intentionally encouraged to practice talking as if they were talking to students, rather than describing the teaching that they imagined doing and using language like "I would say . . ."

Affordances and Constraints of Linking Video Representations with Practice Opportunities The use of a video in this way engages TCs in carrying out the work of teaching. They are positioned to watch a lesson and to "pick up" where the teacher has left off in the mathematics lesson. Meghan and her colleagues have designed an activity in which TCs are positioned to be responsive to ideas that have been shared in the discussion, which is different from viewing and discussing a video of a conclusion to a discussion. At the same time, this is an approximation of practice. TCs are often giving teacher-centered conclusions because they are not able to co-construct the conclusion with students. Further, TCs have limited information about the children participating in the discussion, and thus are limited in their abilities to think about concluding in ways that are attuned to the specific children in the classroom.

CONCLUSION

When selecting a representation to use to support teacher candidates' learning, teacher educators must consider both the type of representation that is a good match with their instructional goals as well as the specifics of the representation that is selected, including the likelihood that the characteristics of the representations are a good match for the group of candidates. As shown across the examples, different types of representations exist: videos, transcripts, decompositions of practice, lesson planning documents, and examples of lesson plans. These representations differ in terms of what they make visible about teaching, as illustrated in the three examples (see table 2.1). While multiple aspects of practice are visible in each representation, it is important for teacher educators to

TABLE 2.1 *Aspects of practice made visible in representations*

	EXAMPLE 1: PLANNING TEMPLATE AND LESSON PLAN	EXAMPLE 2: TRANSCRIPT	EXAMPLE 3: VIDEO
Children's thinking		√	√
Classroom dialogue		√	√
Classroom management			√
Context			
In-the-moment decision making			√
Lesson components	√		√
Lesson objectives & alignment	√		√
Non-verbal interactions			√
Specific teacher language	√	√	√
Teacher elicitations	√	√	√
Teacher's internal decision making	√		
Teacher pacing			√
Teacher tone			√

consider which facets they will focus candidates on during conversations and activities surrounding the presentation of the representation.

Teacher educators must also select a particular representation example to use. Selection considerations include teacher characteristics, the context of the teaching, and the K–12 content in the video. We discuss each of these in turn.

- *Teacher characteristics.* If the representation is a classroom-based record of practice, who the teacher is will have implications for how the representation can be used and for the likelihood that it will support TCs' learning. For example, when selecting a video representation, a teacher educator could select a video which features one of the TCs with whom they are working, a video of a teacher whom the TCs know, or a video of an unfamiliar teacher. Further, there are differences in teachers' experience level and expertise. Expert practice is often challenging to unpack for novices because much of the work being done is invisible, but it can support the novices in developing a long-term vision of accomplished practice. Video of novice teachers may be less expert—by definition—but easier for TCs to envision in their own classrooms.
- *Context of the teaching.* Another set of considerations is the context of the teaching. For example, who are the students? Where is the school located, and are the contexts similar to or different from the schools in which TCs are working? There is no recipe for the ideal context, but different contexts will create different affordances and challenges when using the video with novices.
- *K–12 content in the video.* If the video contains K–12 content, including ideas and practices, the content must be considered. For example, if children are discussing a novel in the video, will TCs need to read the entire novel before watching the video? Similarly, if a teacher is eliciting student thinking around a particular mathematics topic, what types of mathematical knowledge for teaching will need to be clarified beforehand in order to make sure that TCs are positioned to be able to interpret the potential purposes of particular questions as well as the student's responses?

It may seem daunting at times to find a representation that best represents the practice you are working on with candidates. There are affordances and constraints with each type of representation. There may be instances when representations of practice need to be created or edited for the specific course or purpose. What is important to remember is that no representation stands alone. The three teacher educators featured in the vignettes used multiple representations of practice in their courses. For example, Katie Danielson, in the first example, provided four representations of practice for one instructional activity. In addition to considering the type of representation to use in a specific course session, it is important to consider the suite of representations used in the course. This requires teacher educators to consider what is and is not made visible in different representations and to select those that complement one another by featuring different aspects of practice.

The field is still developing resources to use in teacher education, and much work still needs to be done to create representations that are representative of a variety of contexts, content areas, and grade levels. In table 2.2, we provide a list of available online resources that include representations such as videos and lesson plan templates.

TABLE 2.2 *Online resources for representations*

- Annenberg Learner: www.learner.org/resources/browse.html
- Edutopia: www.edutopia.org/videos
- Inside Mathematics: www.insidemathematics.org/
- Teacher Education by Design: tedd.org
- Teaching Channel: www.teachingchannel.org/
- Teaching & Learning Exploratory : tle.soe.umich.edu/
- Teachers College Reading and Writing Project: readingandwritingproject.org/

CHAPTER 3

Modeling as an Example of Representation

Sarah McGrew, Chandra L. Alston, and Brad Fogo

Eleanor, a teacher educator, is modeling discussion facilitation with her students, who are preparing to be secondary English teachers. These teacher candidates (henceforth TCs) are playing the role of high school students and discussing *Narrative of the Life of Frederick Douglass, an American Slave.*

> **Eleanor:** The text begins with Douglass discussing how he does not know his birth date. Why might he begin the memoir this way?
>
> **Jane:** Because it's so common, it's something everyone knows, and the fact that he doesn't kinda shows the problem with slavery.
>
> **Erik:** Right, he could have talked about beatings and stuff, but I think talking about something like knowing when you were born and how old you are shows us something we hadn't considered about how bad slavery was.
>
> **Eleanor:** Okay, so what I hear both of you saying is that 1) it was a calculated decision to begin in this way, and 2) it was done to show us different ways in which slavery was problematic. So I want to push us to consider Erik's statement about why birthdate versus beatings. Consider his audience. Who is Douglass writing to and why might he choose this beginning, given the audience?

The first part of this discussion proceeds as it might in a high school classroom. The teacher poses a question and two students respond, the second one building on the first's comment. Eleanor then draws a comparison between the students' ideas.

In a high school classroom, the discussion might continue from here as students responded to their teacher's comment. Although the TCs are playing the role of high school students, participating in a discussion like this in the context of teacher education is valuable because it offers the experience of being part of a whole-class discussion. Additionally, it demonstrates the instructional materials and moves involved in engaging students in classroom discussion.

In discussions like these in K–12 classrooms, we can only guess at the motives or decision making involved in choosing whether and how to respond to students or when to raise a new question. The cognitive work done by the facilitator often remains invisible. But Eleanor is working to prepare these candidates to facilitate classroom discussions in their own classrooms, so she wants them to understand *why* she is choosing to facilitate as she does. In order to make her thinking visible for candidates, Eleanor steps out of the facilitator's role after responding to the students:

> *Okay, do you see how I repeated and synthesized Jane's and Erik's comments and then posted part of Erik's? I did that to move the discussion deeper around this point of why Douglass began the text with discussing his birth date versus other horrible parts of slavery.*

Eleanor's choice to step out from discussion facilitation offered the TCs a window into her decision making. Marking and decomposing portions of her decision-making process (in this instance and others that followed) helped candidates see inside the discussion to the thinking that guided content selection, creation and use of materials, and pedagogical moves.

Eleanor's strategy of stepping out of the discussion to mark her thinking is a core feature of teacher educator modeling as we conceptualize it. Modeling is perhaps a misleadingly simple term for a complex teacher education pedagogy. Modeling requires the teacher educator to select a complex practice or cognitive skill and then decompose, enact, and metacognitively mark the work so TCs can understand the teacher educator decision making involved in connecting its component parts.

In this chapter, we explore modeling as a teacher education pedagogy. We begin with an overview of the literature on modeling as an instructional practice. We then draw from three examples of how teacher educators use modeling to explore the components of planning and executing a modeling lesson: defining, framing, and conceptualizing the focal practice being modeled; modeling the practice; and debriefing and decomposing the focal practice. We focus on the teacher educator's enactment of modeling and also examine issues related to planning for modeling.

WHAT IS MODELING?

As noted in the introduction, with the turn toward practice-based teacher education, there is a need to investigate the pedagogies that teacher educators might use to support candidates in developing ambitious and equitable teaching practices. Much of the research on modeling has focused on K–12 settings, yet its benefits have helped us see the need for teacher educators to use modeling in preparing TCs as well. The goal of modeling, whether students are K–12 or TCs, is to make complex cognitive work visible so that learners are able to see and begin to take up the thinking and decision making integral to the discipline. Making metacognition explicit is a core feature of modeling with both K–12 students and TCs. One layer of metacognition focuses on K–12 content and skills; a second layer focuses on teacher decision making and instructional moves. Modeling can thus be useful in teacher preparation to help candidates learn to make disciplinary thinking accessible to K–12 students and to make otherwise invisible pedagogical choices visible.

Effective modeling is responsive both to students' needs and to the integrity of the discipline. In modeling, teacher educators represent and decompose disciplinary thinking and pedagogical choices in ways that make the underlying reasoning and values visible. These representations of practice and models of reasoning support TCs in identifying, practicing, and reflecting upon similar instructional moves. Thus, modeling requires enacting the practice, verbalizing metacognition about the processes involved in the practice, and explaining the underlying reasoning for those moves.

The practice of modeling is grounded in a Vygotskyian approach to teaching and learning, based on the principle that all learning is social and dialogic. Research has shown that a teacher's ability to make the "in-visible visible" is an important pedagogical tool to support student learn-ing.[1] Being metacognitive, or reasoning aloud while enacting a practice, is one way to do this. Charles Goodwin demonstrated how experts in various fields use highlighting to support novices in developing the skills, language, and understandings foundational to a field. During highlight-ing, the mentor makes "specific phenomena in a complex perceptual field salient by marking them in some fashion."[2] Metacognition and marking are critical parts of modeling. They help students see inside the complex-ities of the discipline—to the salient features and skills that are founda-tional to and transferable across work within the discipline—and begin to utilize the underlying thinking and decision making.

Research in K–12 contexts suggests that modeling supports students in developing practices and strategies for doing disciplinary work. Cath-erine Snow and Gina Biancarosa's meta-analysis of adolescent literacy re-search identified several forms of explicit strategy instruction as effective in helping struggling adolescent readers improve their literacy skills.[3] Pam Grossman et al. found that middle school English language arts teachers with high scores on a measure of "explicit strategy instruction" were sig-nificantly more likely to have higher "value-added" scores.[4]

Modeling, a form of explicit strategy instruction, is an important com-ponent of equitable instruction. Although modeling is more contested in mathematics education than in the world of literacy, some researchers of mathematics education have argued that simply engaging in mathematical practices may not be enough to support students' learning of these prac-tices.[5] Instead, they contend, "explicit guidance for learning complex skills or ideas is essential if all students are to develop such capacities. Leaving the construction of these skills to chance can make student success suscep-tible to cultural differences in discursive norms."[6] Following on this, Imani Masters Goffney identified "explicit talk" about math language, reasoning, and practices as a key feature of equitable mathematics instruction.[7]

As a pedagogy of teacher education, modeling: 1) makes visible the metacognitive work at the level of K–12 content instruction, and 2) eluci-dates the teacher's pedagogical thinking and decision making. Modeling supports TCs in taking up the language, thinking, decision making, and pedagogical moves needed to make disciplinary thinking explicit and accessible for their K–12 students. We argue that giving TCs access to not only our enactment of ambitious practices but also our metacognitive thinking around those practices can support TCs in teaching in equitable and ambitious ways.

COMPONENTS OF MODELING

At its heart, modeling involves representing an element of practice and stepping out to showcase key points of teacher decision making throughout the practice. It must also involve purposeful framing and debriefs that support analysis of the component parts of the practice and the teacher's choices about the content, context, student needs, and learning goals. An effective modeling lesson with TCs thus requires thoughtful planning and execution. The teacher educator makes several decisions before the lesson, selecting the practice on which to focus and, even more specifically, the parts of that practice to model. During the modeling lesson, the teacher educator defines, frames, and contextualizes the focal practice before launching the modeling. Modeling involves both representing the practice and stepping out to make decision making visible. After modeling, the teacher educator supports TCs as they debrief, discuss, and further decompose the practice that was modeled.

Planning for Modeling

To plan a modeling lesson, a teacher educator must first decide what to model. As in a K–12 classroom, this decision should be based on a number of factors, including the teacher educator's knowledge of students' (the TCs in this case) needs as well as the teacher educator's disciplinary and pedagogical expertise. Not all practices can be modeled during the limited time of teacher education. Practices that may be most appropriate for modeling are those that a teacher will use often in the first years of teaching, or what Deborah Loewenberg Ball and Francesca Forzani call "high-leverage" practices, and practices that are core to the disciplinary work of the content being studied.[8] In preparing to model a practice, a teacher educator should decompose the practice and select aspects of the practice on which to focus. To make this decision, the teacher educator will want to consider the aspects of the practice where new teachers will most need support and those aspects that are more cognitively demanding or complex.

Defining, Framing, and Contextualizing the Focal Practice

In the class session in which the modeling will occur, the teacher educator will want to devote time to preparing TCs for modeling. Because modeling involves candidates playing dual roles—as teachers learning the practice and also (role-playing) as K–12 students—the teacher educator must be explicit about what modeling will look like and prepare candidates for both these roles.

First, the teacher educator will prepare candidates for their role as teachers learning about the focal practice. Teacher educators do this by defining and framing the practice. Depending on how much introduction to the practice TCs have already had, the teacher educator may spend more or less time with this. As noted in chapter 2, modeling may be paired with other representations of practice, including videos or lesson transcripts. Also, depending on the context, the teacher educator may wish to preview some aspects of the practice to which candidates should pay particular attention during the modeling.

Teacher educators will also want to prepare TCs for the role they will play in the modeling lesson as students by contextualizing the modeling: What grade level and subject area is this lesson occurring in? What have students learned leading up to this lesson? What are its goals? Given these, why is the practice being modeled appropriate for this particular lesson? Although it may be brief, this contextualization is vital to prepare candidates to participate in the lesson and to emphasize that the practice being modeled does not exist in a vacuum. Instead, it is an intentional part of an instructional sequence planned based on students' needs. This preview can also directly address issues around authenticity—the ways in which a modeled lesson with adults serving as students might be different in important ways than the same lesson in K–12 classrooms.

Modeling the Focal Practice

Through modeling, the teacher educator represents the practice as a teacher would in a K–12 setting. The teacher educator might facilitate a discussion, cognitively model how to develop a thesis statement, or conference with a small group of students as they work together on a problem. During this representation of practice, the teacher educator steps out periodically to voice the reasoning and decision-making processes that undergird the practice. As in modeling with K–12 students, modeling with TCs should be carefully planned. If teacher educators are modeling a practice that relies on eliciting and responding to student thinking in the moment (e.g., facilitating a small group discussion), teacher educators will not be able to script their modeling. However, they should still have a plan for the reasoning and decision making they wish to highlight.

Debriefing and Decomposing the Focal Practice

After modeling, teacher educators will want to support candidates in debriefing what they experienced during the modeling lesson as role-playing students and as teachers. This reflection and discussion can take many forms, but it should focus on supporting candidates to analyze and understand the planning and decision making that went into enacting the practice. This includes considering the content or skills that were emphasized, the pedagogical moves and the rationale for those moves, and the ways in which the practice supports K–12 students in engaging in disciplinary thinking. The debrief can also give candidates a chance to consider and plan for how they might adapt the practice in their own teaching contexts and how a lesson might unfold differently in a K–12 setting.

VIGNETTES

Decisions are involved for the teacher educator at every step along the way of planning for modeling. In the following vignettes, we offer snapshots of such decision making in practice in history/social studies and English language arts methods courses. The italicized segments in the description of modeling in each vignette are moments where the teacher educators step out in order to make their thinking visible for the TCs.

Vignette 1: Purposeful Planning of What to Model

Our first vignette takes place during the second semester of a disciplinary methods course in a year-long graduate teacher education program. The teacher educator devoted several classes during this semester to facilitating text-based historical discussions. This particular class was focused on the historical question, "Was Abraham Lincoln racist?" Answering this question requires complex contextual thinking as candidates evaluate Abraham Lincoln's views on race in the decades leading up to the Civil War. Before engaging in the teacher educator–facilitated full class discussion, candidates read and analyzed a series of five primary sources, each of which provided nuanced evidence that must be considered within the social and political context of Lincoln's life. Candidates then participated in structured small-group discussions using the Structured Academic Controversy format, in which they worked in pairs and then in teams to explore an issue through opposing positions before trying to reach consensus.

Defining, Framing, and Contextualizing   Prior to modeling the facilitation of a full-class discussion, the teacher educator reminded candidates of the general framework for facilitating historical discussions, which she had introduced in a prior class. Within this broader framework of discussion facilitation, the teacher educator was explicit about her goals for modeling discussion facilitation that day: First, she wanted to demonstrate ways to consistently orient discussion participants to the text, pushing them to ground their claims in specific textual evidence. Second, she wanted to help TCs understand a powerful strategy for organizing discussions on complex questions and supporting students' co-construction of ideas: framing students' arguments, as they emerged, on different sides of pivotal questions within the "Was Lincoln racist?" debate. Finally, she reminded TCs of the grade level and lesson objectives that she had shared earlier in the lesson. The teacher educator then began recording the full discussion to use during the debrief.

Modeling   The teacher educator launched the full-class discussion by saying, "Who wants to begin by sharing where their group arrived in this discussion of 'Was Abraham Lincoln racist?'" A few candidates shared their initial responses, and the teacher educator responded by beginning to frame their comments around one of the central tensions in the document set:

So, I don't want to paint you into corners, but just so we can see: Josie's saying that she's not comfortable taking this term, which is a twentieth-century term, and laying it onto someone in the nineteenth century, and Garrett is like, "Well, it's not that hard for me to do," you know, he sounds like he was racist. You can build from what Josie and Garrett said—I wanted to begin to show the sides of the argument.

The teacher educator's comment was intended to make two participants' disagreement, which represented two possible sides of the debate about whether Lincoln was racist, explicit to other participants. This might help other participants clarify their thinking or prompt the search for additional textual evidence. The teacher educator did not, however, step out to explain her reasons for making this comment. A few minutes later in the discussion, another opportunity emerged for her to frame students' arguments in relation to each other and the central historical question, this time with regard to whether participants were warranted in labeling Lincoln a white supremacist. The teacher educator said:

I have Elizabeth, Stephanie—I want to get to you guys. But, Max just called him a white supremacist, and Andrew very early in the discussion said, "Well, we know he's not a white supremacist." So there's some real disagreement here. [*Did you see how I posted Max's comment and explicitly connected it back to a comment Andrew made early in the discussion? Students might have forgotten that Andrew said that, so I did that in order to draw your attention to one specific question we are disagreeing about. This should get other participants thinking about where they stand on this question of whether Lincoln was a white supremacist.*]

Here, the teacher educator first said what she would normally say to facilitate the discussion, but then stepped out to make her thinking visible. She drew attention to a particular facilitation move—posting students' comments to the whole class—and explained her rationale and objective for the move.

The teacher educator similarly chose moments to make visible her decisions around how to push participants to ground their claims in the text. For example, a participant named Michelle made a comment critiquing the central historical question, arguing that it changed the way she analyzed the texts. The teacher educator responded:

> *I want to pause here and tell you that I am actively balancing wanting to make sure that we all ground our claims in the text, but I also don't want to shut down participation. After Michelle's comment I was going to say, "Was there anything in the text that made you lean one way or the other?" But I thought that might throw you off. So what I'm noting here is as soon as you share I'm going to ask, "Was there anything in the text that swayed you one way or the other?"*

As the discussion continued and delved deeper into an exploration of Lincoln's views, the teacher educator selected a few more moments, based on her goals for modeling, to make her decision making explicit.

Debriefing and Decomposing   The debrief of the teacher educator's modeling of discussion facilitation took place in several stages. First, candidates had an opportunity to reflect individually and discuss in small groups their reactions to and questions about the discussion facilitation. After airing several of these comments and questions with the whole class, the teacher educator moved the class to focus more specifically on the aspects of discussion facilitation that she sought to model. For this portion of the debrief, the class watched segments of the discussion in which they had just participated and reflected on the teacher educator decision making involved in moments of framing participants' arguments and pressing for textual evidence. Finally, the candidates worked in groups to analyze a transcript of a different discussion on the same document set and historical question. Together, they wrote facilitation moves they thought the teacher could have used during the discussion to frame students' arguments and to help them ground their claims in the texts.

Vignette 2: Making Thinking Visible

Our next example comes from an undergraduate teacher preparation program where the methods course focused on the core practices of modeling, facilitating discussions, and using backward design to craft ambitious instruction for middle and high school students. The teacher educator used modeling, coaching with rehearsals, and reflection as pedagogies in her instruction and focused on having students decompose practice and include scaffolding to meet the needs of a range of learners.

Defining, Framing, and Contextualizing   In this vignette, the teacher educator modeled a lesson on detecting irony. The teacher educator chose to model detecting irony with a poem for several reasons. As English majors, TCs often can easily detect and leverage irony in interpreting poetry, but they may overlook places where K–12 students might struggle with this same practice. Candidates also often find it difficult to offer a strategy or process for students to do this work, as these processes have often become implicit for them, or they never learned a strategy themselves. Also, interpreting poetry is complex cognitive work that many K–12 students shy away from and find impenetrable. Hence, TCs can use support in learning how to make this particular kind of disciplinary thinking visible and accessible for students.

The teacher educator presented several accessible examples of irony in everyday life (conversations, comics, political cartoons) and used the examples to elicit the TCs' understandings of irony in order to co-construct a strategy for detecting irony. The strategy was to detect mismatches between what people say and what they mean, what people do and what we expect them to do, or what we know and what the character knows. These mismatches align with different forms of irony that are common in literature.

Modeling   The poem, "Hazel Tells Laverne," was printed in large font on chart paper and read aloud by a volunteer. The teacher educator explained that she would model how to use the strategy of detecting mismatches in order to find the irony in the poem and begin to make sense of the poem's overall message. She then launched into her metacognitive marking and think-aloud using the strategy:

> Now I want to use our strategy of finding mismatches to detect irony
> in this poem and use those moments of irony to better understand

the poem. First, I want to consider the genre. Poetry. What do I know about poems? I know that they are often not meant to be taken literally; poets are careful with what language they use; words may have double meanings or be repeated for emphasis.

So, as I read this poem, what I get in a summary is that Hazel and Laverne must be janitors at a hotel. And she's telling her this story about a frog in the toilet. Where's the mismatch? Is there a mismatch between what is said and meant? No, I think she really means there was a frog in the toilet that was talking about her being a princess. I think the frog means what he says, too.

Is there a mismatch between what she does and what I expect? Well, sort of, I mean here (*marking the text*) when her mouth drops open it's about being a princess, not that there's a talking frog in the toilet. That is different from what I would expect. I would expect her to be freaked out when the frog pops up and starts talking—not by *what* he says but that he's in the toilet and that he's talking.

Is there a mismatch between what I know and what the characters know? Yes. I remember the story *The Frog Prince,* and in that story, a girl kisses a frog and he turns back into a prince. So that might be the bigger point of irony or mismatch. I know that fairy tale and Hazel doesn't—and that's what makes this ironic. And perhaps that's the point the author wants us to focus on. [*Do you see how I used our process of detecting mismatches to figure out what's ironic in the poem?*]

Now the question is, why does she want us to focus on that fairy tale? [*Remember it's not about simply finding the mismatch but then beginning to think about why the author included that mismatch—it's on purpose, and what is that purpose?*]

So if the author wants us to think about that fairy tale, let's do that. What else do I know about the fairy tale? The girl in the fairy tale was already a princess, I think, so that's different. Hazel is no princess, she's a janitor in a hotel, and she keeps repeating that phrase in the poem . . . "me a princess." For me this is another sort of mismatch. [*Do you see how I used my prior knowledge of this fairy tale that the author is alluding to?*]

I know that in poetry, repetition means that it's there for emphasis. And I note that here (*marking text*) it's "me a princess" and then the last time there's a line break, which is also important in poetry (*marking text*), and here it's "me/ a princess." So, there is a mismatch between the girl in the fairy tale and the girl in this story. One's a princess whose kiss turns a frog back into a prince, and here it's a working-class woman cleaning a hotel restroom who flushes him down the toilet.

Now, I want to think about the "so what." Why would the author want me to think about this? What are the big ideas, takeaways, etc., that the author wants me to engage with?

At this point, the teacher educator stopped modeling and asked the class to gather in small groups to think about this "so what" question. After working in small groups and discussing their ideas about the irony in the poem, TCs were given a different text in which to investigate and analyze irony.

Debriefing and Decomposing   To begin the debrief, the teacher educator asked the class to think about the moves she made in the lesson, focusing their attention on her selection of skills, strategies, texts, materials, and lesson structure, as well as her pedagogical moves and possible motives. She put up a slide with questions to guide the debrief:

- Why might I have chosen to model detecting irony?
  In a poem?
- What did you notice about my language during my
  modeling? What about the underlining?
- Consider the structure of the lesson and where the mod-
  eling takes place. Why were you involved in the process
  to develop the strategy but not in using the strategy with
  the poem?
- After the modeling, what happens next in the lesson plan?
  Can you see the instructional scaffolding and gradual release
  of responsibility? How and when do I use these strategies?
  Why do you think I structured the lesson in this way?
- What do you notice about the selection and progression of
  texts used in the lesson?
- What else did you notice? What questions do you have?

The teacher educator's goals during the debrief were to make explicit the intentionality behind the selection of the content and skills, demonstrate how modeling can fit into a larger lesson design, and draw attention to the use of thinking aloud and metacognitive marking during the modeling. Many of the TCs noted during the debrief that they were hesitant about teaching poetry and that, although they could find irony easily in a text, they paused when thinking about how to teach someone else to do that work. At this moment, the teacher educator emphasized that her knowledge of them as students helped her to select content in ways that supported and pushed their learning. She emphasized that modeling works best when selecting practices and content where explicitness can make complex cognitive work more accessible, thus offering students greater opportunities to learn.

Vignette 3: Framing and Debriefing Modeling

Our next example of modeling comes from a semester-long methods course for secondary history/social studies candidates. The course was organized around disciplinary approaches to teaching history, and in particular, inquiry and critical literacy. In this particular class, the TCs worked through a document-based lesson featuring primary and secondary sources highlighting different perspectives and accounts of what happened during the first encounter between Aztec Emperor Moctezuma and Spanish Conquistador Hernán Cortés. The teacher educator used the lesson to model the practice of cognitively modeling source analysis.

Defining, Framing, and Contextualizing   The objectives for this particular class were to observe, consider, and practice examples of cognitive modeling and guided practice. The teacher educator began by sharing a definition of and justification for the practice of cognitive modeling. He stressed that modeling and guided practice are important strategies but difficult to do well, and that there are different ways to use them for different purposes and in different contexts.

The teacher educator then provided context for the day's lesson, explaining that it would take place in a tenth-grade world history classroom as part of a unit on the Columbian Exchange. The lesson focused on the questions: What happened when Moctezuma met Cortés? Did Moctezuma think Cortés was a god? The student objectives were to investigate the first encounter between the Spanish and the Aztecs in 1519, and to observe and practice source analysis. Finally, the teacher educator specified questions for candidates to consider while they participated in the lesson: How are skills introduced and modeled? Where are opportunities for students to practice the skills? What scaffolds are present? He also asked candidates to consider how the students at their teaching placements might participate in the lesson and interact with the materials used that day.

The teacher educator then transitioned into the role of classroom teacher and led the candidates through the lesson. The first part involved reading a short textbook account of Moctezuma meeting Cortés and considering how it helped them understand this event. In pairs, candidates read the textbook excerpt, identified its claims, and discussed the limitations of the account.

Modeling Next, the teacher educator explained that the class was going to continue investigating the first encounter between Moctezuma and Cortés by reading and analyzing two accounts of this event. He directed TCs to a document titled "Cortés's Letter to King Charles." He then began modeling by holding up the document and saying:

> So, this is evidence. And today, we are going to be reading and analyzing this piece of evidence and using it to help us address the questions: What happened when Moctezuma met Cortés? And, did Moctezuma think Cortés was a god?
>
> One skill that we use when analyzing historical documents is sourcing. When sourcing a document, we ask, before even reading the document: Who wrote the document? When did they write it? Who was the audience? And, what was the purpose for writing the document? This type of source analysis helps us to analyze historical evidence and documents. This is important because by considering these questions, we can begin to determine the credibility or reliability of a document, before we even start reading it. [*I want to pause here to note*

that the first thing I've done in this modeling is to define the skill that I'm modeling—sourcing—and to provide a rationale for it.]

So what I am going to do now is to show you how I might source this document (*placing the document under a document camera and bringing it into focus*). While I am doing this, I'd like you to follow along and annotate the document in the same way that I do.

Okay, let's begin. Document A: Cortés's Account. (*reading*) "In his letter to King Charles, Cortés describes meeting Moctezuma and claims that Moctezuma told the following story about the origins of the Aztec people."

Now, the first thing I want to do before reading the document is to consider its source. (*reading*) "Source: Letter (*underlining "letter"*) by Hernán Cortés (*underlining "Cortés"*) to King Charles V (*underlining "Charles"*) written in 1520" (*circling "1520"*). [*I want to pause again and draw your attention to the design of the materials: Do you notice how the source information is clearly identified on the document? It is also included at the bottom of the page, which requires some nonlinear reading to focus on as an initial step in our analysis.*]

This is important information. First, I notice the author is Cortés. It is, therefore, a firsthand account (*writing "firsthand account" under Cortés's name*) as Cortés was obviously present at this event. And I notice that it was written in 1520, which was one year after Cortés met Moctezuma. This means it was written relatively soon after the event (*writing "written soon after meeting" below the date*). The fact that this is a firsthand account written soon after the event makes me think that this might be a good piece of evidence for our investigation. [*Again, I want to pause to point out that I'm analyzing the source aloud and also modeling for students how they can mark up a source note by taking notes like I am.*]

But I also want to think about to whom Cortés is writing. And I see it is King Charles V, who is essentially Cortés's boss (*writing "boss" underneath King Charles V*). This makes me wonder, why is Cortés writing? If Charles is funding Cortés's expedition, perhaps Cortés will want to stress his accomplishments, and he might exaggerate a bit to make it sound like things are going well (*writing "stress accomplishments?"*

and "exaggeration?" below Cortés's name). This makes me question the document a bit. I also realize that this document comes from the Spanish perspective (*writing "Spanish perspective"*) and I am wondering how Cortés understood Moctezuma. How was this translated? (*writing "translation?"*). [*Another pause here as I want to just note how sourcing, in this instance, involves beginning to consider the credibility of the document in relation to the inquiry's central historical question.*]

Okay. So, by sourcing the document, I understand that it is a firsthand account of Cortés meeting with Moctezuma written soon after the event. This makes me think that, on one hand, it might be a trustworthy account. On the other hand, I realize that it comes from Cortés's perspective of this event, that he has somehow translated Moctezuma's words, and that he is writing to his boss, the king. This makes me question the credibility of this document a bit. As I begin to read the document, it is important to keep this source information in mind as I continue to analyze it as a piece of evidence for our investigation.

After the modeling, the candidates engaged in two guided practice activities of source analysis. In the first, they read the text of the Cortés letter with a partner and answered guiding questions, which focused both on considering the document's source information and on closely reading the document. They then analyzed another document, an excerpt from the *Florentine Codex*, through addressing and discussing a similar set of sourcing questions.

Debriefing and Decomposing   The candidates began debriefing the lesson with a freewrite followed by a pair share. The prompt for this activity was: What are your impressions of this lesson? How was thinking modeled in this lesson? Where were opportunities for guided practice? Next, the teacher educator built upon the class discussion with a series of slides aimed at identifying key components of the modeling lesson. He structured this decomposition of practice with a series of slides titled: "Framework for Planning and Executing a Modeling Lesson." This framework was broken down into three parts: into, through, and beyond, which were respectively organized around the questions: How do we prepare ourselves and our students for a modeling lesson? What do we do during a modeling lesson? What do we do after the modeling? He then shared different elements of instruction that he employed across each of the phases.

DISCUSSION

The vignettes above draw attention to critical features of modeling: in all three cases, the teacher educators carefully selected practices, skills, content, and materials that are both central to the discipline and cognitively complex. In making these choices, they attended to the particular needs of their TCs and the K–12 contexts in which those candidates taught; they made thinking visible during enactment by stepping out of the practice to voice their reasoning in concise and precise language; and they led carefully planned debriefs. We argue that each of these features works in concert to support TCs in learning to make complex content accessible to a range of learners.

In each vignette, the teacher educators selected practices to model with candidates and those candidates' K–12 students in mind. They selected high-leverage practices that candidates should develop understanding of in order to have a foundation upon which to build as they gain experience and expertise. Further, each focused on complex cognitive work with which K–12 students often struggle: making text-based claims and co-constructing ideas in classroom discussion, identifying and analyzing irony in poetry, and conducting source analysis of historical documents. In this way, modeling a practice with TCs was used to help those candidates understand how to support all students to engage in complex cognitive work.

Moreover, each teacher educator modeled a practice within the larger context of a classroom lesson. This involved positioning TCs as students and taking time to share details about the context within which the lesson might be situated. For example, the teacher educator in the third vignette helped candidates imagine the classroom setting into which they would be stepping by detailing the grade level and unit as well as lesson objectives. Such framing helps candidates understand how practice is connected to lesson and unit objectives and bracketed by activity structures to help introduce and extend practice. Candidates also experienced the activity structures surrounding the modeled practice. In the first vignette, TCs (acting as students) analyzed sources and participated in structured small group discussions before engaging in the modeled full-class discussion. In the second vignette, candidates worked through an anticipatory set of examples illustrating the concept of irony before the modeling, and then worked in small groups after the modeling to practice detecting mismatches in another text. In each of these cases, candidates had opportunities to engage in disciplinary thinking that were structured throughout the lesson. This was designed to help them see how the practice that was modeled served to support students in developing that disciplinary thinking.

Teacher educators and candidates were not limited to their roles as K–12 teachers and students. Central to modeling is making one's thinking visible *during* the enactment of the practice. Stepping out and attending to the cognitive work underlying the practice opens up access to that cognitive work so that candidates do not miss what the teacher is doing and why. In each vignette, the teacher educators stepped out of their role as classroom teacher to highlight key moments for TCs. In the first and third vignettes, metacognitive marking was focused at the level of explaining the teacher educator's instructional moves and decisions. In the first vignette, the teacher educator stepped out of facilitating the discussion to draw attention to her decisions about when and how to intervene in the discussion. These moments were selected based on the specific parts of the practice (framing students' arguments and orienting students to the text) on which the modeling was focused. In the second vignette, metacognitive marking was focused at the level of explaining disciplinary content and skills for K–12 students. In this case, the teacher educator shared a practice for detecting irony based on mismatches in a poem; moments where she stepped out were designed to help candidates understand ways in which they might support students in accessing and developing disciplinary skills. In all the vignettes, each moment of metacognitive marking began with a statement like "Do you see how I just . . ." or "I want to pause there . . ." in order to mark the shift in roles and position candidates to consider this metacognition not as K–12 students but as teachers.

While the teacher educators in these vignettes made cognitive disciplinary work visible by explicitly voicing it, they did not launch into lengthy metacognitive monologues. Instead, they limited the reasoning they shared while stepping out to just a few sentences of clear and concise explanation or rationale. In the third vignette, the teacher educator provided brief explanations about pivotal moments of modeling source analysis at four different points, highlighting critical features of cognitive modeling like defining and providing a rationale for the practice. In each of these cases, the reasoning he shared was concise (just one or two sentences) and directly related to the goal of his modeling.

Each vignette provided examples of debriefs where TCs returned fully to the role of teachers and worked together to unpack the component parts of the practice that was modeled. These debriefs, which one teacher educator referred to as "taking off the student hat and putting on the teacher hat," shared the goal of unpacking and interrogating the teacher educator's choices as a teacher. Teacher educators used individual reflections, small- and large-group discussions, and teacher educator–led summaries to support candidates in decomposing elements of the modeling. Teacher educators focused on the sequence of materials and activities, the scaffolding provided to support students to engage in complex thinking, and teacher moves and decision making. While teacher educators primarily relied on small- and large-group discussions to draw out these elements, they sometimes directed a portion of the debrief, as when the teacher educator in the third vignette used slides to review the major elements of planning and facilitation "into, through, and beyond" the modeling lesson. Finally, these debriefs maintained a consistent focus on how candidates might use and adapt the practice that was modeled with their own students.

Modeling as a pedagogy must be combined with other representations, opportunities for decomposition, and chances to practice. Each of these vignettes was followed by opportunities for TCs to design, practice, and receive feedback on enacting the practice that was modeled. For example, following the modeling lesson on poetry analysis, volunteers rehearsed making their metacognition explicit with the poem in front of their peers, receiving coaching and feedback from the teacher educator along the way. In addition, TCs were asked to develop and enact a lesson in which they modeled a specific English language arts strategy in their field placements. The TCs videorecorded their lessons and reflected on their use of the instructional strategy. Candidates engaged in a similar sequence after the other modeling lessons, including participating in rehearsals of the practice that was modeled, trying out the practice in their teaching placements, completing structured reflections, and providing feedback to peers. In this way, modeling served as a powerful pedagogy of teacher education to help develop teacher candidates who can teach in equitable and ambitious ways.

CHAPTER 4

Approximations of Practice in Teacher Education

Kristine M. Schutz, Pam Grossman, and Meghan Shaughnessy

In this chapter, we explore the use of various types of approximations of practice that teacher educators can use to support novice teachers. Approximations represent an opportunity to engage in aspects of practice with additional support and under conditions that are designed for optimal learning.[1] Approximations generally try to target specific elements of practice and create conditions of reduced complexity, in order to make it easier for professionals to try out new elements of practice while reducing the consequences of failure.

Many professions use approximations of practice during professional education. Law schools use moot court to enable law students to develop courtroom and litigation skills; medical schools increasingly use simulations of many kinds, such as simulated emergency scenarios or physical simulations of surgical techniques, to enable medical students and doctors to develop clinical skills without involving actual patients. Airline pilots practice in flight simulators to learn to take off and land large aircraft without risking passengers. In clinical experiences, dental students are given opportunities to work with real patients, with careful consideration of the difficulty of the situation. They encounter more complex cases over time as their skills develop. Examples of approximations used in teacher education include role-plays; microteaching; rehearsals; virtual reality simulations, such as TeachLive; and other structures that enable novices to enact the role of a teacher in a setting that is designed to support learning.

Approximations of practice provide opportunities for novices to enact the role of the professional; rather than discussing how a teacher *might* react to a particular student comment, approximations push novices to actually try out that response. In contrast to teacher education modeling, described in the previous chapter, which generally has novice teachers observing a teacher educator's teaching and enacting the role of students, approximations require novices to take on and enact the role of teacher. By focusing on teaching enactment, approximations provide novices with the opportunity to have the visceral experience of responding in the moment and to receive immediate feedback from peers and teacher educators.

Approximations also provide opportunities to "decompose" or break down the different elements of complex practice and enable novices to focus on particular elements prior to integrating all of the different elements at once.[2] Medical students, for example, often learn to take patient histories without necessarily conducting a full physical examination. Taking a history is only one element of conducting an exam, but it represents a critical element. Getting it right, listening for the stories patients tell and the symptoms that provide diagnostic clues, is a challenging component of practice that is worth focusing on. Similarly, in teaching, giving concrete, actionable feedback to student writers is an element of teaching practice that requires focused attention. It requires novice teachers to review student writing and listen closely as writers describe their process and product, and use the information gathered to determine the focus of the feedback and degree of scaffolding they will provide. Approximations help novices try out and refine components of complex practice prior to "recomposing" these elements in the full complexity of classrooms.[3]

Approximations range along a continuum from less to more authentic with regard to the full complexity of practice. Student teaching might be considered the most authentic approximation of practice, since it takes place in actual classrooms with K–12 students, and the student teacher assumes most of the responsibilities of a classroom teacher. However, it is still an approximation because the student teacher does not have full responsibility for the classroom. Role-plays with peers, in contrast, are less authentic, since they don't involve K–12 students and generally do not involve novices in managing a full classroom.

As this description makes clear, approximations can take place in both university and K–12 settings. Some forms of approximation, such as simulations or role-plays, happen most frequently in the context of university-based coursework, while (by definition) coteaching with mentor teachers and student teaching takes place in school settings. Approximations in the context of university classrooms enable teacher educators to focus on enactments of practice that can then be taken up in K–12 settings. In rehearsals, for example, teacher candidates (henceforth TCs) typically rehearse a practice or instructional activity that they will then be enacting with K–12 students; in this instance, the connection between the rehearsal and the experience enacting teaching in classrooms with students is transparent.[4]

Authenticity, however, is only one dimension of approximations. Less authentic approximations, such as role-plays or rehearsals, offer opportunities for in-the-moment feedback and do-overs that are more difficult to include when teaching in front of students. For example, when novices learn to provide instructional explanations or engage students in choral counting in mathematics, they often need support with the content, including questions to pose to students and how best to respond to student questions. In a rehearsal, which is an approximation, the novice teacher or the teacher educator can pause to consider what a student's question might mean or address confusion around the content, and then restart the rehearsal to allow the novice to try again. It is important to note that in this scenario, everyone involved in the rehearsal, whether enacting the role of teacher or not, can learn from the feedback.

A critically important component of approximations of any kind is the debrief paired with the approximation. In work on medical simulations, the debrief is considered the most critical component, as it allows medical students and doctors to reflect on both what went right and what went wrong, and to identify areas for improvement. The debrief allows teacher educators to make visible subtle or not so subtle aspects of complex practice that may not yet be apparent to novices; for example, when TCs begin approximating facilitating discussion, they may not be aware of who is having opportunities to talk and who is not, or the extent to which their use of closed questions deflects more open-ended responses. The location and structure of the debrief varies across approximations. In rehearsals, for example, discussion and coaching occur as the teacher educator or candidates pause teaching; at the conclusion of a rehearsal, many teacher educators revisit key learning extracted from the pauses to help novices prioritize feedback.

In developing approximations to use in teacher education, there are a number of issues for teacher educators to consider. First, teacher educators need to consider the specific elements of practice that are being targeted. Are we asking TCs to approximate very specific skills, such as wait time; a core practice, such as eliciting student thinking; or instructional activities, such as choral counting or writing conferences, that might include multiple core practices?

Teacher educators also need to decide on their role in the approximation, as well as the roles of all of the TCs, including those who are enacting the role of the teacher, those who are simulating students, and those who may provide side coaching or support. In preparing novices for approximations, it is important to make these role distinctions clear and to provide guidance for what it means to enact a particular role.

Part of this role clarification involves making clear who can provide feedback and the nature of the feedback to be provided. In our own work with rehearsals, we have found it helpful to identify ahead of time a set of decision rules for pausing a rehearsal to provide feedback. For example, a teacher educator could decide to pause when there is an opportunity for the teacher to immediately use the feedback to try again, to pause to provide feedback if there are inaccuracies in content, and to pause when moments of practice can be highlighted in order to help teachers see concrete examples of ambitious instruction.

In addition to considering the elements of practice being approximated and the participant roles being enacted, teacher educators should also pay attention to the tools that support novices during approximations.[5] In our own work developing and using approximations in teacher education, we have found it useful to ask the following questions to determine the tools necessary for supporting TCs as we plan for approximations:

- How will TCs know what they are aiming for inside approxima-tions? What kinds of representations will the teacher educator use to support candidates in developing a common language for and vision of the element(s) of teaching practice TCs are approximating?
- How will TCs be supported in planning for the approximation? Will they receive a detailed and supportive planning tool? A scripted lesson? Will they coplan or plan individually? How is the level of support influenced by the requisite content knowledge necessary to engage in the approximation, the complexity of the facet of practice being approximated, and the level of experience of the TCs?
- What can be constrained in the approximation as an additional way of reducing complexity? Will everyone use the same text, task, or problem? Will candidates plan with the same instructional goal in mind?

In the sections that follow, we provide concrete examples of different forms of approximations and explore the kinds of learning opportunities they provide for TCs. In each example, we look at how the teacher edu-cator addressed the issues raised above, and we detail the kinds of norms and resources that are required to create these kinds of approximations in the teacher education setting.

UNIVERSITY-BASED APPROXIMATIONS OF TEACHING PRACTICE

In spite of increased calls for capitalizing on clinical experiences to sup-port novice teachers in learning to teach, many methods courses still occur in university classrooms with limited opportunities to engage with children in K–12 classrooms. Incorporating approximations of practice into university-based methods courses is a powerful way to situate candi-dates' learning inside practice and begin to address what Kennedy terms "the problem of enactment."[6] By providing structured and scaffolded ways of "trying on" teaching, we can begin to develop novices' capabilities to simultaneously engage with content and students in ways that leverage the resources that individual children bring to their learning. In this way, we are engaging novices in learning to teach in ways that are responsive to the rich diversity of ideas and ways of participating that children bring to instruction. In the sections that follow, we describe and share examples of four university-based approximations used by different members of the Core Practice Consortium in their university-based methods courses.

Approximations Tied to Video Extensions

Many teacher educators share video representations of classroom teaching with novices to begin to develop a common vision and common language to describe practice. Video can also be a useful tool to design approximations of practice. Beyond sharing and analyzing video, teacher educators can design experiences that use the video as the stimulus to create opportunities for candidates to consider how they might respond. Video extensions occur when a teacher educator shows a video of classroom teaching practice, pauses the video, and asks novices to respond in the role of the teacher. The ways in which teacher educators structure the task of responding can differ from simply having candidates turn to a partner and say how they would respond, to more complex tasks where a teacher educator might ask candidates to gather together to plan the remaining part of the lesson and then enact the plan for the class.

A peek inside teacher educator practice. In Kristine Schutz's upper elementary literacy methods course at the University of Illinois at Chicago, she uses video extensions to support novices in learning to facilitate discussions. Specifically, she uses the approximation to help TCs develop skills and language for orienting children to one another's ideas within text-based discussions. In reviewing videos of TCs' assigned teaching, Kristine noted that most novices, eager to give as many students as possible an opportunity to share, collect many responses to questions they pose to students. However, the novice teachers needed support to help children connect their ideas to one another's in order to co-construct meaning of the text. To address this, Kristine outlined a number of talk moves that teachers can employ to support students in connecting and building on peers' contributions.[7] She defined each move, shared sample language, and asked students to brainstorm other possible language. This is because the goal is not to use the language provided "word for word." Rather, the goal is to understand the intention of the move and to be able to phrase it in specific ways that connect with learners in classrooms. After introducing the talk moves, she then had students read the text *Coral Reefs*, by Joanna Solins,[8] in preparation for the video extension approximation. Just as teachers read and analyze texts before teaching in classrooms, TCs need to engage in the same process. Deep comprehension of the text enables TCs to anticipate the potential misconceptions and resources that students potentially bring to the discussion. She then shared a video of a teacher leading a discussion about the text and stopped at predetermined moments to have TCs determine what they would say next. She selected these moments by previewing the video of the discussion and identifying moments in which children needed support co-constructing meaning. Below, we share an excerpt of Kristine's plan for this video extension in which she identified the stopping point, and shared a possible interpretation of the student's contribution, some purposes of the teacher's next move, and suggested language for one of the purposes.

When the video was stopped, TCs were prompted to consider what they would say next. During the first few stopping points, Kristine provided candidates with two minutes of think time and then had them share their next response with a partner as she listened in. For later stopping points, she asked candidates to immediately turn to a partner and take on the role of the teacher to share how they would respond. After each stopping point, Kristine would rewind the video and let novices see how the teacher responded and how the response influenced the next few moments in the discussion. She would then stop the video again to discuss how the teacher's move compared to the moves the TCs had tried on. Kristine's purpose for the comparison was not to have novices check the accuracy of the moves they had tried. Instead, she endeavored to help novices see how different teacher responses can steer discussions

FIGURE 4.1 *Excerpt from Kristine Schutz's video extension plan*

STOPPING POINT	FOCUS
12:52—After De'Andre says: *Yeah, it's really sad that because of careless divers and fishermen who don't seem to care about the ocean, we might lose these really cool looking reefs.*	What we notice about his response: • Attends to the part of the text about careless divers and fisherman. Might only understand part of the cause of the deterioration of the coral reefs. (Possible that he just shared part of his thinking and does understand the role of other factors as shared by his classmate and in the text.) • Does not connect to the previous (Adrian and Adela's) comments about the impact of pollution. Possible purposes of teacher response: • Elicit further thinking. • Prompt the class to turn back to the text. • Prompt class to consider how De'Andre's contribution relates to Adrian and Adela's. Possible language for third response: • How does what De'Andre just shared about the carelessness of humans relate to what Adela and Adrian were saying (about the impact of pollution)? • How does that connect with what Adela and Adrian were saying?

in various ways and delve into the reasoning behind why teachers might select one move over another to support specific learning goals.

Approximations tied to video extensions make use of a representation of practice, a classroom video, as a springboard to engaging TCs in an approximation. In chapter 2, which focuses on representations of practice, the authors described another example of how Meghan Shaughnessy used a video of a mathematics discussion as a springboard for focused work on concluding a mathematics discussion. In this approximation, TCs (1) engage with solving an elementary mathematics task that is going to be focal in a mathematics discussion and anticipate children's solutions to the task, (2) view a fifth-grade discussion of solutions to the mathematics task where the principal focus is understanding the different approaches taken by students, stopping the video right before the discussion conclusion, and (3) take on the role of the teacher and conclude the discussion with peers serving as students. Similar to Kristine's example, Meghan sought to have TCs consider the different purposes that a teacher might have for concluding a mathematics discussion (such as highlighting a particular pattern of student thinking, or tying off the discussion so that it can be returned to on a subsequent day). This particular example highlights the deliberateness with which teacher educators need to select video representations if they are seeking to use them for a video extension activity.

Video extensions allow TCs to engage in the immediate and contingent work of teaching, which is responsive to the ideas that have surfaced and cannot be preplanned in a lesson plan. It also enables TCs to discuss the purposes behind the decisions that they make, and to help them connect techniques to purposes. Because the approximation is paired with a representation of practice, it also provides novices with authentic representations of students and their ideas. The discussion around the utility and impact of the instructional decisions TCs make in the approximation is valuable in helping candidates develop principled decision making inside practice. One limitation is that novices cannot see how students in the video would respond to their moves, but—as we argue about representations—no approximation is complete, but must be paired with additional opportunities to learn in and from practice.

Approximations Using Fishbowls

cool!

Most of us recognize a fishbowl as a participation structure used in many K–12 classrooms to support students in seeing an interaction from multiple perspectives, but it can also be a useful structure for approximations in teacher education. Fishbowls provide TCs an opportunity to experience teaching practice from the perspectives of teacher, student, and observer. During a fishbowl approximation, novices form two concentric circles. In the inside circle, one novice is assigned the role of the teacher, while the other novices take on the role of fictional students. Novices in the outer circle are given specific observation tasks and roles to support their noticing. For example, half of the novices in the outer circle might document the questions a teacher is asking while facilitating a discussion, while the other half records student contributions. During the fishbowl, the teacher educator can participate in a variety of ways, including joining the inner circle as a fictional student, pausing the inner-circle action to highlight teacher moves the candidate is making, or observing from the outside circle to support the facilitation of a constructive debrief for novices following the experience. TCs can rotate through the multiple roles throughout the approximation as well, enabling them to experience practice from multiple perspectives.

A peek inside teacher educator practice. In her work on justice and equity issues with novice teachers at the University of Washington, Sarah Schneider Kavanagh designed and used an approximation using the fishbowl structure to support candidates in enacting interactive read-alouds. She used the interactive read-aloud as a vehicle through which she addressed issues of representation and equity.

A central challenge to equity-oriented teaching is that certain groups of individuals are often not represented in the curricular canon. And when marginalized groups *are* represented in books and curriculum, students often respond in prejudiced ways that display the assumptions and bias they carry, and teachers need to manage the disruption of such beliefs. As a teacher educator who cares deeply about justice and equity, Sarah sought a way to support novices in figuring out how to integrate content about groups, peoples, and communities that have been traditionally marginalized by mainstream society, and how to disrupt and transform assumptions and bias when revealed by students.

To begin to help novices learn to engage in this critical work, Sarah identified and outlined a set of practices to help novices begin to address prejudice inside instruction.[9] These included:

- Introducing counternarratives
  - Explicitly interrupting marginalizing social narratives
  - Implicitly interrupting marginalizing social narratives
- Anticipating students' prejudice
- Responding to students' prejudice

She introduced these to TCs by naming and defining the practice and then providing an example. For instance, when discussing the practice of introducing counternarratives by implicitly interrupting marginalizing social narratives, she talked about how a teacher might share a story about a man who is the primary caretaker of a child. Because it is a strong social narrative that men are not primary caretakers of children, telling a story about a man who serves in this role implicitly interrupts the existing social narrative.

Sarah used a fishbowl approximation to support candidates in learning to enact these practices as they facilitated interactive read-alouds using the text *Stella Brings the Family,* by Miriam B. Schiffer.[10] She deliberately selected this text because it offers a counternarrative about family structures, as Stella has two dads. In advance of the approximation, Sarah worked with TCs to deepen their understanding of the narrative the story interrupts, and to emphasize the importance of interrupting that narrative, both broadly in our society and for the children in the classes they will teach. Under her guidance, the candidates discussed how same-sex families are rarely represented in society, and how there is a dominant social narrative that all children have a mother and a father. Sarah drew TCs' attention to the fact that it was important to anticipate that many children in the class might hold this marginalizing social narrative. As such, she worked to co-construct a plan for how they would activate children's schema about families and family structures when launching the read-aloud. Together, they decided to begin by showing children the cover of the book, a picture of Stella and her two dads, and saying, "Today we're going to read a story called *Stella Brings the Family.* Look closely at the cover. Who are these people on the cover?" The class anticipated that children would respond in a number of ways, but that it was very likely that some children would assume that it was Stella, her dad, and another relative or friend, as many children would not assume that it was Stella and her two fathers. Asking questions that surface children's assumptions would thus create a space to begin to enact the practice of responding to students' prejudice. Through this preparatory planning, Sarah helped candidates begin to see how they could anticipate prejudice and pose questions that surfaced children's unrecognized bias.

After completing a plan for the interactive read-aloud with TCs, Sarah used the fishbowl to help novices learn to enact the focal practices of leading an interactive read-aloud while teaching. Consistent with the fishbowl structure, Sarah formed inner and outer circles of participants. In the inner circle, one candidate acted as the teacher, facilitating the interactive read-aloud of *Stella Brings the Family,* while a small group of candidates played the role of primary-grade students. Candidates in the outer circle were divided into two groups. The first group's task was to observe for the practices they had discussed in class and raise a sign when they noticed the practice being enacted. Each member of this group had a sign with a different practice written on it—introducing counternarratives, explicitly interrupting marginalizing social narratives, implicitly interrupting marginalizing social narratives, anticipating students' prejudices, and responding to students' prejudices. So when the "teacher" asked the "children" who they thought was on the cover, the observer with the *anticipating prejudice* sign raised it for everyone to see. The second group of candidates in the outer circle were each assigned a practice and tasked with creating a public record on a whiteboard of what the teacher was saying or doing when the practice was enacted during the approximation. This enabled the group to develop a record of practice to analyze during the debrief of the teaching. During the approximation, Sarah often contributed as a student, drawing from her knowledge of biased remarks children might unknowingly make, in order to provide comments that were ripe for the rehearsing candidate to attempt to use the practices they had discussed. For example, when the teacher posed the anticipating prejudice question discussed above, Sarah immediately acted the role of a student and responded that it was a picture of Stella, her brother, and her dad, thus prompting the teacher to attempt to respond in ways that disrupted the dominant social narrative.

Sarah used the fishbowl as an approximation to help candidates see, name, and experience how the practices are enacted inside teaching. She viewed the creation of the public record as a necessity in helping novices come to understand what practices look like when enacted, as opposed to only understanding what is represented in a lesson plan. Through the use of the public record in the debrief, she was able to use direct quotes from the approximation and help candidates see how they attempted to interrupt assumptions and bias in different ways, see the impact of these attempts, and consider other ways they could have addressed pedagogical dilemmas around prejudice in the approximation.

The fishbowl structure provides a space in which TCs see and experience practice from multiple perspectives, that of teacher, student, and observer. Like rehearsals, fishbowls provide a space where candidates can engage in the interactive work of teaching, and teacher educators can make student contributions that appropriately anticipate and represent student thinking with which TCs may not yet be familiar. These targeted contributions prime the TCs to enact specific practices or moves that have been previously introduced by the teacher educator. Finally, the work of the outer circle requires novices to begin to see teaching through a particular lens and to document their observations. These observations support both the teacher educator and the novices in developing a common language to describe practice during the debrief.

Partially Scripted Simulations

Approximations of practice may vary with the degree of predesigned scripting. In clinical psychology, instructors often create role-plays with an initial script for an interaction between client and therapist in order to prompt novice therapists to encounter particular problems of practice.[11] In our experiments with partially scripted simulations in teacher education, two TCs enact the role of a teacher and student while a third novice serves as a record keeper, taking notes that accurately represent how the teacher-student interaction unfolds. The teacher educator provides a script for the "student" to guide initial teacher-student interactions. When designing the script, the teacher educator intentionally creates opportunities for TCs to try on ways of interacting that are within their zone of proximal development. As novices become more skilled, knowledgeable, and experienced, the teacher educator can design the scripted student responses to call for more sophisticated interactions and teacher moves. This type of approximation seems particularly appropriate in situations where the candidates are simulating one-on-one interactions between a teacher and a student. This approximation can be used in a whole-group or small-group setting. In what follows, we describe how Kristine Schutz used partially scripted simulations in her early elementary literacy methods course at the University of Illinois at Chicago.

A peek inside teacher educator practice.   Kristine used partially scripted simulations to support novices in learning how to prompt beginning readers when they have difficulty reading a word. Prompting is complex work that requires teachers to draw on their knowledge about the reading process, and to make hypotheses about how students are making sense of a text as they decode, all while considering the linguistic demands of the word and the level of support the reader needs at this time. In her experience working with novice teachers, Kristine had noticed that novices tend to rely on the prompts from their own experiences learning to read, for example, telling a student to "sound it out." This prompt often falls flat as it rarely matches the linguistic demands of the word and the resources the reader brings to the text. For example, telling a child to sound out the word *right* is not an appropriate prompt because the word *right* is phonetically irregular. Instead, a teacher might prompt the child by saying, "Look for parts you know." Thus, Kristine realized that TCs needed scaffolded opportunities to try out different prompts. Although Kristine could have asked TCs playing the role of the student to just showcase the same sorts of challenges they would anticipate children would have, she also knew that most of the TCs she taught had little experience working with beginning readers. Thus, she needed to support them in providing realistic student responses as well as support their developing ability to anticipate common challenges.

As such, Kristine, in collaboration with Emily Machado, a graduate student instructor, selected a text appropriate for an early reader and scripted how the "student" would read the text—where they would hesitate, words they would substitute or omit as they read, places where they would reread the text or appeal for help from the teacher. This enabled the teacher educators to create opportunities for TCs to prompt. Kristine and Emily deliberately made initial opportunities more obviously connected to specific prompts, while later opportunities in the text could be addressed with a number of prompts and required more sophisticated decision making on the part of the novice. They also indicated the challenges the student would face using annotation marks the TCs had previously learned for taking running records.

Leading up to the partially scripted simulations, Kristine engaged TCs in multiple activities designed to deepen their specialized knowledge for teaching reading, including conducting, analyzing, and interpreting assessments such as running records; and watching small-group reading lessons where teachers prompted individual readers when they got stuck on a word. On the day the class would participate in the partially scripted simulations, Kristine asked novices to share prompts they had heard teachers use with beginning readers. Consistent with her past experiences, many candidates shouted out, "Sound it out!" and were surprised to hear that there were other prompts that might be more generative and targeted to support beginning readers. Kristine then shared a prompt list[12] with the class, providing examples on a document projector and talking through when each prompt would be appropriate.

Kristine then used partially scripted simulations in two ways, first as a whole-class simulation to introduce the approximation and begin to develop a set of principles for prompting, and then in small groups to provide all TCs with an opportunity to take on the roles of teacher, student, and recorder.

During the whole-class simulation, Kristine displayed the text on the document projector and followed the script that she had created, making intentional miscues TCs would need to prompt as she read, and responding to candidate prompts as she anticipated a beginning reader would. Teams of novices were assigned the teacher role for different pages, and Kristine encouraged novices to use the prompt list she previously shared to support their prompting. For example, the actual text Kristine was reading said: *The tow truck pulled the car.* However, when Kristine read it out loud for the TCs, she pronounced tow with a diphthong (i.e., rhyming with cow). One candidate tried using the prompt, "Look for parts you know." Kristine read the text again, repeating the miscue she had previously made. Another candidate attempted to prompt saying, "Try a different sound," and Kristine then read the text as intended. Once Kristine got to the end of the page, she stopped the class to discuss the successful and unsuccessful prompts, and to support candidates in understanding how teaching children to vowel flex—trying different sounds that vowels or vowel digraphs make—can be a helpful strategy. The class continued with the simulation until a number of TCs had tried prompting. Following the simulation, Kristine asked what they had learned from the prompts their peers used, and she helped the class develop a running list of principles to support prompting. These included:

- Keep language concise and direct.
- Match your prompt to what the child needs to do or attend to.
- Keep prompts general.
- Wait. Let the child try to problem solve.
- Prompt to build independence.

After the whole-class activity, Kristine prepared novices to engage in the same activity in their small groups. Within the group, each novice took on one role—teacher, student, or recorder. Teachers were told to prompt students as they read a marked-up version of the text, showing them where and how to get stuck while reading. Students applied their knowledge of the running record annotation marks to read the text as determined by the teacher educator, and they responded in the role of the student when the teacher prompted. The recorder took detailed notes of the reading and prompting, so the teacher and student could look back on the documentation to accurately recall the interaction and determine how appropriately matched the prompts were to the challenge the student reader faced. As novices worked in groups, Kristine circulated and coached the simulations. Upon completion, Kristine facilitated a debrief of the experience, once again putting the text on the document projector, talking through specific examples with TCs, and adding to the list of principles for prompting. The class rotated through three short texts, thus enabling each candidate to rotate through each of the three roles.

Through partially scripted approximations, teacher educators boost TCs' understandings of genuine ways in which students experience instruction, and the resources and misconceptions they bring to their learning. This contributes to candidates' developing knowledge of students, and it enables them to begin to identify patterns and trends in student thinking. One could imagine a partially scripted approximation being used in a variety of disciplines, where instead of scripting how a student reads a text, a teacher educator could script certain understandings and misunderstandings that a student brings to the instructional interaction. For example, in science, this could be a misconception or understanding about a scientific phenomenon or in English language arts, it could be a students' interpretation of a text. In each of these cases, the TCs would practice eliciting student thinking to develop an understanding of what the student knows.

K–12 CLASSROOM-BASED APPROXIMATIONS

In the last decade, there have been a number of calls for increased clinical experiences for preservice teachers and job-embedded professional learning opportunities for practicing teachers. Yet, it is important for us to consider the quality of these experiences, as opposed to simply the frequency. We believe that clinical experiences and job-embedded professional learning require deliberate attention and structure to adequately scaffold teachers' learning and that structuring these experiences as approximations of practice, where complexity is intentionally reduced to allow for focused and deliberate practice inside classrooms with actual students, can greatly support novice learning. Approximations that limit the scope of what is being approximated through coteaching or pausing the flow of teaching to allow extra time and support for processing and determining how to respond to students are possible ways to scaffold such experiences. In this section, we share short examples of these two classroom-based approximations, which we term *deliberate coteaching* and *processing pauses*.

Deliberate Coteaching

One approach to designing approximations of teaching in K–12 classrooms is to create deliberate coteaching experiences either with teacher educators (i.e., course instructors, field supervisors, instructional coaches, and mentors) or colleagues. We argue that these experiences must be intentionally designed to support novices' needs. Coteaching experiences that are not collaboratively preplanned with articulated roles, responsibilities, and ways of interacting within lessons do not provide sufficient scaffolding for TCs to be labeled approximations. As we design such experiences, we need to consider things like: What does the novice need to get better at? How can we structure the coteaching to allow close focus on this particular aspect of teaching? How will a plan for teaching be constructed that enables the coteaching participants to understand instructional goals and the lesson flow? Deliberate coteaching allows TCs to center their focus on one specific aspect of practice or part of teaching, observe more experienced teaching practice, and collaborate with colleagues to plan.

A peek inside teacher educator practice. Recognizing the challenge of engaging novice teachers in investigation-based science teaching, Betsy Davis, a teacher educator at the University of Michigan, sought to devise a structure to help TCs enact investigation-based science teaching with support. As such, she designed a teaching experience for TCs that enabled them to teach a "small slice" of a lesson while a mentor taught the other parts. Betsy began by introducing the candidates to a three-part science lesson. She guided them through in-class activities to build their understanding of each of the three parts—experience, engage, and explain and argue—and their relationship to one another. She then explained that they would teach the "experience" portion of an investigation-based science lesson to a whole class or small group of students in their field placements, and their mentor teachers would teach the other components of the lesson. Betsy explained to TCs that this assignment would give them the chance to focus on and teach only the part of the lesson in which students would collect data. She stressed how this part of the lesson has many moving parts and how it is helpful, as a novice, to practice this portion on its own. Candidates identified a science lesson plan with their mentors based on the guidelines in figure 4.2, analyzed it, and then developed a full plan using the three-part structure in collaboration with the mentors.

Betsy provided TCs with an instructional planning template intentionally designed to help novices plan three-part science lessons, and she shared an annotated version of the template with candidates for extra planning support. TCs coordinated with their mentors and cotaught the lesson, with candidates launching the lesson with the "experience" part

FIGURE 4.2 *An excerpt from guidelines articulated by Betsy Davis to support novices in selecting a lesson*

This lesson must involve an opportunity for students to *experience a natural phenomenon* (e.g., conducting an investigation about light, mixtures, living things, weather, or rocks and minerals). Some examples, across grade levels, that could work well include:

- using pulleys to measure how they make work easier
- experimenting with celery stems to see how water flows through them
- dissecting owl pellets to analyze the types of bones to explore the owl's diet
- observing evaporation and condensation to determine when these processes occur
- testing materials for their electrical conductivity
- doing a simulation of predator-prey relationships

Some lessons work less well for these assignments, because they don't involve collecting and/or analyzing data to make sense of a phenomenon and construct an explanation about it. Examples might include constructing (but not collecting data on) different forms of structures, sorting photographs of plants and animals, doing initial measurements for a year-long investigation, researching biomes, learning how to use a new science tool, playing science-related games, or singing science-related songs.

and then seamlessly shifting the responsibility for the "engage" and "explain and argue" parts to the mentor. TCs then analyzed video of the portion they taught according to guidelines Betsy provided.

Many teacher educators structure other types of experiences where novices are supported in learning to teach through the use of deliberate coteaching in classroom settings. For example, many of our colleagues who serve as field instructors coplan and coteach lessons with TCs in their field placements. A field instructor might support a TC in planning for a guided reading lesson based on formative assessment data collected through running records, then have the TC only teach the subset of the lesson where students read independently, and the teacher circulates to provide individualized feedback and coaching to individual readers. What makes these coteaching opportunities deliberate is the attention to the structure, roles, and responsibilities of each teacher in both the planning and enactment. It differs from other useful conceptions of coteaching where teachers build upon one another, often interrupting to elaborate or clarify for students without intentional preplanning.

Deliberate coteaching experiences offer TCs opportunities to delve deeply into one aspect of practice while contextualizing this aspect in a full lesson. When planned for and implemented with intention, these experiences have the potential to serve as approximations and representations of practice as the TC both enacts and observes teaching. Candidates can see how students take up what they say and do inside their teaching and compare this with their mentor's interactions with students. Further, because the TC and mentor have coplanned the lesson, the mentor potentially serves as an informed guide and support—there to support candidates as they focus on newer aspects of practice.

Processing Pauses

Another approach to designing approximations of teaching in K–12 classrooms is to structure teaching to allow for processing pauses, moments where the instructional interaction freezes and TCs stop to consider how they will proceed in consultation with a teacher educator or peer. We know that responding to pedagogical dilemmas in a principled way in the moment is challenging for novices, as it requires them to draw from and integrate multiples sources of knowledge within the fast-paced swirl of classroom life. As such, it's important for teacher educators to consider approximations where we slow down practice to provide novices with time, space, and support to develop responsive teaching practice.

A peek inside teacher educator practice. Elizabeth Dutro teaches an undergraduate writing methods course at the University of Colorado Boulder. This course is embedded in a school setting, and Elizabeth has developed a relationship with a second-grade teacher in which TCs are paired with student writers with whom they work each week throughout the semester. Elizabeth designed a mediated field experience for TCs to help them learn to assess student writing and give feedback during writing conferences.

Supporting teacher candidates in learning to conduct writing conferences that require teachers to quickly analyze student writing, determine an instructional goal, and confer with children in a single moment is complex. In her years of experience, Elizabeth recognized that TCs often had difficulty with the rapid pace of writing conferences. As such, she developed a mediated experience to allow space for candidates to process and collaborate with others while learning to confer. Elizabeth mediated the experience through the creation of a three-part activity structure for learning to confer, where TCs first meet with student writers to review and discuss their writing, in what she refers to as a "flyby." The candidates then step away from the student writers to discuss possible instructional goals with a teacher educator and peers, and later return to enact the writing conference with the student writer. Prior to the flybys, Elizabeth introduces TCs to the structure for the writing conferences they will enact. She further supports the initial information-gathering interactions by providing a protocol for the flyby and guiding candidates in planning for the interaction using a structured planning template. In this planning template, novices craft potential questions they could use during the flyby based on their previous knowledge of the student's writing (see figure 4.3).

FIGURE 4.3 *Elizabeth Dutro's structured planning template*

Based on your observations and interactions during independent writing on March 14, what stage of the writing process is the child engaged in? (pre-writing, drafting, revising, editing, publishing)

Plan for the following (write information where indicated by boxes)

I will begin the conference with open-ended questions.

My first question will be:

Other questions I could ask during this initial part of the conference (list 2–3 additional questions):

Elizabeth further assists planning and enactment by sharing a supporting document that outlines the structure of the writing conference and contains suggested language to use during the enactment (see figure 4.4). After the flyby, TCs gather to collaboratively consider how they will move forward when they return to continue the conference. In addition to using teacher educators and mentors as thought partners, TCs also reference streamlined documents Elizabeth has created to bolster their knowledge about writing traits and strategies. Candidates make decisions about the focus and methods they'll employ in the conferences, and then return to the student to enact teaching.

In this approximation, TCs analyze the writing of students they have consistently worked with in the course, making it more authentic to the classroom practice. However, unlike writing conferences that classroom teachers conduct, candidates are provided with additional time and support to review the student writing and plan their responses. This enables TCs to process the information they have gathered about the writer and

FIGURE 4.4 *Writing Conference sample questions crib sheet*

Talk *with* students about the work they're doing as writers. (What is their intent, and how are they going about it?)

- Invite the student to set the agenda:
  - How's it going?
  - What are you doing today as a writer?
  - What do you need help with today?

- Read the student's writing (or excerpt), or have the student read:
  - What's the big idea of your piece?
  - What are you trying to do?

- Respond to the piece of writing as a reader:
  - I really liked . . .
  - As a reader, I was confused by . . .

- Identify a teaching point:
  - Support the writer's intent.
  - Connect to mini-lessons you have recently taught.
  - Select an area of focus that is best for the student.

Your role: Help the student become a better writer . . . NOT to improve a particular piece of writing.

the writing, and then collaborate with others to identify an appropriate course of action. Given that many TCs are still acquiring the specialized knowledge for teaching writing, the support they receive from teacher educators (course instructors and mentors) often provides them with adequate knowledge to bolster their teaching of writing. As TCs take on more responsibilities in classrooms, they will need to do this analysis and planning in real time with student writers. This approximation begins to provide candidates with experiences they will engage in as teachers, yet contains scaffolds to support their learning.

Kristine implemented a similar approximation when working with practicing teachers who were encountering similar challenges while conferring with student writers. However, instead of having the teacher step away from the student, teachers teamed up in groups of three, and an entire triad would be present as one of the teachers launched the conference with the student writer and gained a sense of what the writer was doing well and where they needed support. When the teacher had gathered sufficient information, the conference was paused, and the three teachers discussed their thinking about how to proceed in the conference. They worked together to identify a specific strategy to support the writer. Once they came to agreement, the teacher reengaged in the conference, and the other two teachers continued to observe. Should the conferring teacher need support at any time, the conference could again be paused for conversation with the team. Because teachers had expressed having an inadequate understanding of writing strategies, Kristine had also worked with the teachers to develop a "cheat sheet" containing eight possible conference ideas and suggested teacher language that they carried with them and referred to when making decisions about how to proceed.

GETTING STARTED WITH USING APPROXIMATIONS
Principles for Selecting and Designing Approximations

In selecting or designing approximations to support novice teachers, it's worth spending time thinking through the practices that are particularly important for TCs in a given program to be able to enact skillfully as beginning teachers. With the limited time available in most teacher education programs, instructors will not be able to focus on and provide practice opportunities for all aspects of teaching; the identification of high-leverage practices in the University of Michigan's undergraduate elementary teaching program can be seen as one response to this challenge. Articulating a small set of core practices that are central to a course or program will help focus the selection of approximations.

A second principle for identifying practices to approximate has to do with their degree of challenge. Leading a whole-class discussion, for example, is a particularly challenging practice with multiple components. It calls upon teachers to serve as facilitator, elicit student thinking, listen carefully to and track student ideas, orient students to each other's ideas, track the development of ideas across turns, and provide a productive conclusion to the discussion. None of this is easy. Developing a sequence of approximations which allows TCs to tackle one component of the overall practice—such as eliciting student thinking—followed by approximations in which they try to weave together student ideas helps address the challenges experienced by novices.

A third principle for using approximations requires that teacher educators develop a shared understanding of teaching, specifically of the activities and practices that TCs will approximate. In our own work, we have found the work preceding approximations to be particularly important in helping candidates understand what we are aiming for inside approximations. We have found it useful to use multiple representations of practice including—but not limited to—video representations, teacher educator modeling, planning templates, and lesson plans to support candidates in decomposing and understanding fine-grained aspects of practice that are within their reach as novices. Chapters 2 and 3 in this volume provide examples of the ways teacher educators incorporate the use of representations to help TCs understand the components of practice.

When we move approximations to K–12 classrooms, we must also consider how to involve mentors and other practicing teachers in co-constructing a shared vision for practice. We have found it helpful to engage in shared activity as a larger community of practice to construct a collective understanding of practice. These activities typically involve engaging all partners in decomposing representations of practice that align with the specification of practice we are using to support TCs. For example, we help mentor teachers to see and understand not only how we decompose the practice of facilitating discussion into its constituent parts, but what this might look like and how it might change over time in novice development. Watching video representations of practice together can also support this shared understanding.

A fourth principle for adapting or designing approximations has to do with the power of pausing to provide feedback. The "pausability" of approximations is part of what makes them such a generative learning opportunity for TCs; being able to pause in the midst of an instructional explanation, for example, to get feedback and then to try again rarely happens in classroom settings. For this reason, it's well worth investing in approximations that provide such opportunities for in-the-moment feedback and do-overs. Many teacher educators feel uneasy with the idea of pausing teaching because it feels uncomfortable to interrupt. Previewing for candidates how to anticipate the feedback occurring within approximations can diminish this discomfort. The teacher educator will of course need to think through this in advance to consider when and how to pause teaching, and how to ensure that the feedback provided is useful to both the TC enacting the lesson and to those who are observing or participating in the student and observer roles. For many of us, pausing teaching as it unfolds in K–12 classrooms raises questions about how it will potentially impact the classroom dynamics and subsequent instruction. It is likely that in the context of a classroom, there would be fewer pauses than we might expect in approximations in university classrooms. In our experiences pausing to support candidates during instruction, we find it helpful to raise K–12 students' awareness as to how these moments support their teacher's learning and consequently their own. It is also important to establish norms with both students and classroom teacher about how to handle such pauses. With appropriate norms and guidelines, it can be empowering and valuable for the K–12 students we teach to see their teachers positioned as learners and striving to become better at what they do.

Ways into Working with Approximations

Many of us are new to integrating approximations of practice into our teacher education classrooms. Unlike the modeling of lessons by teacher educators that is a ubiquitous feature of teacher education classes, approximations of practice, particularly those that take advantage of the ability to pause practice, are still relatively rare. So we understand from our own experiences the challenges of trying to run rehearsals, simulations, and other approximations for the first time. We encourage teacher educators who are new to this to start small. The use of video extensions or partially scripted simulations or role plays may build on practices already used in the classroom, and may also provide an opportunity to bridge into further opportunities for TCs to enact components of practice. In our own work, we've found that shifting from having students discuss a video to taking on the role of the teacher at a particular point to respond to a particular scenario can be enlightening for TCs and teacher educators alike.

As with introducing any new activity structure, it is important to be clear about the purposes, guidelines, and norms associated with the approximation. Moving from talking about what they might do as teachers to actually being asked to take on the role of the teacher to respond to a scenario can be challenging for TCs at first; they may also react to the inauthenticity they feel serving as the teacher of their peers. Addressing directly the value of trying out the practices they will later use with students with their peers and asking that everyone take the approximation seriously will help set the stage for engagement. Our own collective experience has shown us that TCs, as well as experienced teachers, deeply value the opportunity to try out new practices in the relative safety of an approximation, even if there is initial resistance. We have also found it helpful to provide a model of a rehearsal or other approximations, so that TCs understand the roles they're being asked to take on and the purpose of the pauses and feedback.

When experimenting with a new approximation, we also encourage honesty with the TCs about the effort involved in trying something new. This allows the teacher educator to model the role of teacher as learner. Finally, when experimenting with new approaches to bring approximations into university coursework and professional development spaces, it can be useful for teacher educators to find colleagues who are willing to support and provide feedback on those efforts. One of the biggest gifts of the work of the CPC has been the opportunity to share our practice with colleagues both inside and outside of our institutions and to receive feedback that helps us develop our own practice.

CONCLUSION

We believe that incorporating approximations of practice as opportunities for novice teacher learning is an important and critical component of professional preparation and continuing development. Approximations provide a space in which teacher candidates can enact components of practice—whether in university classrooms or K–12 classrooms—in ways that can be intentionally scaffolded to attend to teachers' development and the challenges of responsive teaching. Moreover, within approximations, teacher educators and teacher candidates have opportunities to engage with specialized knowledge for teaching and the principles of equity-centered instruction in contextualized, meaningful ways. As this chapter has illustrated, there are multiple ways to incorporate approximations of practice into teacher education. In the following chapter, the authors provide a more extended example of rehearsals as a particular form of approximation.

CHAPTER 5

Rehearsals as Examples of Approximation

*Megan Kelley-Petersen, Elizabeth A. Davis, Hala Ghousseini,
Matthew Kloser, and Chauncey Monte-Sano*

INTRODUCTION

Within a given moment of instruction, a teacher simultaneously manages the disciplinary content being taught and the students' engagement, both with each other and in relation to the content. Because these complex interactions happen within the same moment, we consider the teacher educator pedagogy of *rehearsal* to be a powerful resource to support teacher learning and practice. Rehearsals are one way of approximating teaching practice in teacher education (or other professional development settings). A rehearsal becomes a shared experience for a group of teachers and teacher educator(s) to practice—just as professional athletes practice—in order to be better positioned to manage the range of complex interactions within a lesson with students. As we have employed them, rehearsals typically last between ten and twenty-five minutes, where at least one teacher educator supports at least one novice teacher to publicly try out a part of a lesson with fellow teachers playing the part of students. Throughout this chapter, we frame rehearsals as occurring between a teacher educator and teacher candidates (henceforth TCs). However, colleagues have also used the practice of rehearsals in their professional development learning experiences to support practicing teachers' learning and development. While our descriptions and explanations highlight TCs' learning, we also see merit in using rehearsals as a teacher educator pedagogy to support any teachers' learning. A teacher educator supporting practicing teachers through rehearsals will likely need to consider adapting the descriptions and details in this chapter to better meet the context and learning needs of practicing rather than preservice teachers.

A teacher educator planning a rehearsal with a group of TCs must consider a range of purposes and goals for the rehearsal, considering the contexts relevant to the TCs as they work *into* the rehearsal. Working *through* a rehearsal, the TC publicly enacts a lesson, lesson segment, or set of instructional practices, trying out the focal moves for this enactment. At some point during the enactment, the teacher educator may initiate a *pause* to stop the action. Some discussion ensues, either directly between the teacher educator and the TC or involving the whole group. When appropriate, the action starts again and the TC resumes the enactment (either replaying a portion or starting from where the enactment left off). Multiple pauses can occur within the entirety of the rehearsal. When the rehearsal is completed (or time has run out), the enactment portion ends and typically a debrief occurs, providing an opportunity to move *beyond* the single rehearsal into greater and more generative opportunities for participating TCs to learn.

We begin this chapter by highlighting the work of the teacher educator within each part of a rehearsal by unpacking the *into*, *through*, and *beyond* of rehearsals. We then offer insights into making the pedagogy of rehearsals work in various contexts for teacher learning. Throughout the chapter, we draw from various academic content areas to illustrate the broad applicability of this type of approximation of practice.

MOVING *INTO* A REHEARSAL: IDEAS FOR HOW AND WHAT TO PREPARE

As with all teaching, facilitating successful rehearsals takes preparation. Public displays of work are often reserved as culminating activities in educational settings, performed after students have developed some expertise. In addition, teaching is often done in isolation, and TCs have likely not observed teaching as a public act. So preparing novices to share their practice and cultivating a culture of inquiry into that practice takes concerted effort. Teacher educators must consider several factors that contribute to a productive learning environment in which TCs are willing to take risks as they try new things and develop a more complete understanding of instructional practices that support their students.

Defining structure and roles

The teacher educator makes numerous decisions when setting up an effective rehearsal; these are ideally driven by the goals of the rehearsal and knowledge of the TCs, their contexts, and their needs and readiness as learners. A teacher educator must decide whether to conduct whole-class or small-group rehearsals or some of each. When conducting whole-class rehearsals, teacher educators will ideally select which TCs rehearse and in what order, choosing TCs early on who will maximize learning for all candidates. To be fair, these choices should be communicated to the TCs ahead of time. When having small-group rehearsals, it is helpful to gather volunteer teacher educators to lead each group, and to think about how to prepare those volunteers.

Teacher educators will also want to identify a particular segment of a lesson that will be rehearsed, rather than an entire lesson, as well as identifying what areas of work to highlight in the teaching practice that is targeted by the rehearsal. In many of our practice-based methods courses, rehearsals have tended to follow a period of time spent on a particular core practice, so teacher educators can focus candidates on a narrower part of instructional practice. In addition, the teacher educator's understanding of children and youth and how to support their learning can guide what is emphasized during rehearsals. The chapter appendix highlights a structure and protocol for rehearsals and possible areas of emphasis.

Identifying norms

Identifying and sharing norms for rehearsals is an important first step that lays out ground rules for how the group will work together effectively. One example of norms is shared in figure 5.1. Of note is the immediate and direct attention to the work of teaching rather than to evaluations of particular TCs. This norm highlights that the purpose of rehearsals is to improve collective understanding of the teaching practice that is being rehearsed, and the skills that are needed to support student learning. This set of norms also clarifies the roles of the teacher educator and TC

FIGURE 5.1 *Norms for conducting rehearsals*

- When we discuss teaching, we are not here to evaluate people ("good" or "bad"). Our focus is on the work of teaching and what teachers try to accomplish in order to support student learning.

- Comments need to be respectful to both students and teachers. Try to pose critical comments in the form of questions.

- The teacher or teacher educator can ask for a pause to make a comment, ask a question, or provide a suggestion about an aspect of practice we are working on.

- When you are playing the role of a student, it is good to have humor but try not to exaggerate what students will do.

Source: From p.6 of the "Rehearsal Primer" by Kazemi, Kelley-Petersen, and Lampert, LTP Project (tedd.org).

as participants who may pause the rehearsal and comment, or ask for or provide feedback. And for nonrehearsing TCs and teacher educators who play the roles of students, these norms give us a reminder to not let the role-playing distract from the main focus of the rehearsal.

In one literacy methods class, a teacher educator and another volunteer teacher educator first modeled a five-minute rehearsal in order to illustrate these norms and what a rehearsal that abided by these norms looked like. One person played the role of the rehearsing TC and one played the teacher educator. The person playing the rehearsing TC purposefully made moves that prompted the teacher educator to pause and provide suggestions, make comments, or ask questions. The commentary was intended to show respect for the TC, and to keep the focus on inquiring into practice rather than evaluating the rehearsing teacher. This model set the stage for upholding and reinforcing norms throughout subsequent rehearsals.

Establishing a common purpose

A central purpose of rehearsals is to understand and improve the enactment of practice in order to support student learning. Conducting rehearsals—as opposed to enacting instruction for the first time directly with K–12 students—provides the space for reflection, troubleshooting, collaboration, and revision in a way that live teaching does not. Teacher educators can clarify the purpose of the rehearsal in a set of guidelines to review before rehearsals begin. Rehearsal guidelines can be used to guide TCs' and teacher educators' attention and thinking during and after the rehearsal. We have used guidelines to shine a spotlight on key areas of work in the targeted core practice being rehearsed so that TCs and teacher educators remain focused on the work of teaching. For example, in one social studies methods course TCs were asked in a handout to look for the following areas of work to guide rehearsals of discussion facilitation with visual texts:

- Planned questions and discussion moves elicit student thinking and help students build understanding of the learning goals and central inquiry question.
- Questions are open-ended but target the learning goals or central inquiry question and attend to key details in images.
- Discussion moves support students in listening, responding to, and building on each other's ideas.
- Discussion moves help students use details in the visual texts to support their thinking.

These points become the lens through which TCs consider what is being rehearsed and what will be discussed after the rehearsal (e.g., What do TCs notice about these areas of work? What questions do they have, or what do they take away from the rehearsal with regards to these areas of work or the practice as a whole?). An elaborated version of rehearsal guidelines is shared with TCs in the course and with volunteer teacher educators who may be leading rehearsals in small groups of TCs (see chapter appendix "Our goals"). Alternatively, teacher educator(s) and TCs can collaboratively create guidelines for their rehearsals as a part of their norm setting and community building. If providing preestablished guidelines feels prescriptive, then we suggest establishing the guidelines collectively. Regardless of how guidelines are established, having clarity around these norms and guidelines highlights core areas of work embedded in the practice targeted by the rehearsal, reinforcing the purpose of understanding and improving enactments of a core practice.

Anticipating key issues

We have found that it is important to give TCs time to develop their teaching materials with feedback before rehearsing, so that the rehearsal can focus on the *enactment* of practice. Given the dearth of strong curriculum materials across content areas, we have found that without this guided preparation time, rehearsals can devolve into problem-solving and improving the curriculum candidates use, rather than on the actual enactment of a practice. Therefore, considering the lesson materials candidates will use and giving them time to develop those as necessary *before* the rehearsal can be an important move as a teacher educator. Another option is to have candidates use ready-made, high-quality curriculum materials where available.

Seeing TCs' lesson materials can provide teacher educators with a way to anticipate subject matter issues as well as student learning issues that could arise during rehearsals. For example, in facilitating rehearsals of discussion facilitation with visual texts, a number of subject matter issues could arise: Do the texts present contrasting perspectives? Do the texts include proper attribution? Does the central inquiry question align with the texts? Does the candidate appear to understand the topic and represent it accurately? In the same rehearsal, issues related to student learning and thinking might arise: Are the texts and any adaptations to them age-appropriate? Do the texts give students the opportunity to think about the central inquiry question in a rich way? Does the candidate track students' thinking visually in a way that supports students' collective thinking? The particular subject matter and student learning issues will likely depend on the particular lesson being rehearsed, but are central considerations in feedback on practice, since the purpose of learning the work of teaching is to support student learning about the subject matter.

MOVING *THROUGH* A REHEARSAL: CONSIDERING WHEN, HOW, AND WHY TO PAUSE

Vignette: Supporting the range of teacher candidates

Erica was rehearsing the discussion portion of a lesson in Kevin's science methods course. She paused herself once, early in the rehearsal, to give some context she thought was needed for her rehearsal. Then, four minutes into the rehearsal, Erica asked the question, "Who can tell me just what this graph is showing us?"

After a bit of wait time, one of the TCs, acting as a student, responded to Erica's question; Erica started to respond. At this moment, Kevin asked if he could ask Erica to pause by saying, "Can I pause you for a second?"

Kevin went on to ask, "What is it that you really want from the question you asked?" Kevin and Erica's conversation that ensued identified that her question was ambiguous: it might indicate that she just wanted students to note the purpose of the graph, but it might instead indicate that she wanted her students to begin actually interpreting the data.

In response to Kevin's question about the intent, Erica said, "I wanted them to say 'sea level change versus year.'" Kevin said that he almost answered with an interpretation of the data, which was quite complex.

Kevin went on to note, if one takes a data-interpretation meaning of the question, then "that's a big question to drop right at the beginning." Erica asked, "So if I said, 'What is the purpose of the graph? What is it trying to show us?'" Kevin noted that this combination of questions (using "purpose" along with "show") would do a better job of steering the students toward her intended purpose, which was to stay at a high level for now with regard to the goal of the graph. Once this was resolved, Kevin quickly said "Go" and Erica seamlessly moved back into her discussion with her students, incorporating this suggestion into her next statement.

Planning for pauses

As part of moving into the rehearsal, we recommend identifying in advance a small set of foci that are considered fair game for pausing a rehearsal. Typically, these would center on the core practice at hand. For example, in the vignette above, the candidate is rehearsing how to facilitate a sensemaking discussion in science, so the pauses focus on issues related to leading a discussion (e.g., how to ask a productive question, or how to support students in building on one another's ideas). That means that many potentially relevant foci are off the table. For example, classroom management moves or how the teacher is writing on the board might be considered inappropriate as a focus for a pause, but might be reasonable to comment on in the debrief after the rehearsal. The teacher

just like in our rehearsals?
Choose what to address!

educator needs to determine the within-bounds foci for the rehearsal in advance. Some teacher educators consider some crosscutting issues to be always grounds for a pause. For example, a teacher educator might always reserve the right to pause a candidate's enactment if the representation of the content is inaccurate or if an equity issue arises. Whatever the guidelines for pauses, these should be clear to everyone.

Another decision for the teacher educator to make in advance, and to share with TCs, is who is allowed to initiate a pause. Some teacher educators prefer to only initiate pauses themselves. Some allow the TC who is rehearsing to initiate a pause. And some allow any TC in the group to initiate a pause. Each of these approaches has an underlying rationale. In our experience, the teacher educator is most likely to initiate a pause, and in only a few cases does the rehearsing TC do so. It is even less likely that other candidates in the group would pause a colleague to stop the action—even if they are technically allowed to do so. (Indeed, the norms presented in figure 5.1 and the associated vignette assume that only the teacher educator or rehearsing TC can initiate a pause.) A related decision is who can join the discussion during a pause. Because of the ways in which rehearsals are intended as learning opportunities for *all* participating candidates, we recommend that teacher educators encourage the participation of all group members in discussion during a pause.

When moving through the rehearsal, a pause can occur for many different reasons.[1] For example, a pause can serve to highlight something important, but can also be an opportunity for the teacher educator to provide feedback to the rehearsing candidate, or a chance for the group to problem-solve around an issue. In addition, a pause can allow a teacher educator to ask for a rewind (i.e., to ask the rehearsing candidate to try something over again). We have also seen pauses used early in a rehearsal to provide important contextual information (e.g., the intended grade level or previous experience of the students) or, later in a rehearsal, to support a candidate in managing his or her time. A pause can also have different substantive foci,[2] such as when the intent is to stabilize or correct the content, or to decompose the practice into more manageable chunks. The pause can also attend to student thinking, the activity structure, student engagement, classroom management, language, a shared referent, or a set of conceptual tools. Finally, a pause can support how to actually enact a move with students.

Enacting teacher educator roles and moves

Pauses can take different structural forms that reflect different roles for a teacher educator.[3] For example, the teacher educator can give directive feedback, give evaluative feedback, scaffold enactment, and/or facilitate discussion. Often, when teacher educators are scaffolding enactment, they take on the role of a student or of a teacher. When teacher educators provide directive feedback, they might provide specific directions for a move to make next, or provide a range of possible productive options: "Try a turn-and-talk now" or "Try asking students why that works, as this is important to understand." A teacher educator might find it helpful to highlight particular moves and draw all TCs' attention to the nuanced or complex aspects of teaching practice by giving evaluative feedback: "That question might confuse students," or "That was a thoughtful way to position students as sensemakers." Since rehearsals become space for TCs to simultaneously balance learning pedagogy and content, a teacher educator might scaffold the enactment by playing the role of a student in order to provide opportunities for TCs to practice responding to both correct or incorrect student responses. Additionally, a teacher educator might scaffold enactment by briefly taking over the role of the teacher in the rehearsal and modeling a move for the TCs. Finally, a teacher educator can engage the entire group of TCs in a short reflective discussion within a rehearsal in order to support the rehearsing TC: "What could we do next here, and why might that be a productive move?" or "How can we think about supporting students who are English language learners in this moment of the lesson?"

Considering challenges

A challenge for the teacher educator is knowing when to intervene—in other words, when to initiate a pause. Our recommendation is to initiate a pause only when doing so would help to meet some of the teacher educator's purposes. Most importantly, pauses should focus on the practice being worked on in the rehearsal and the core foci identified in advance.

Beyond this key idea, our research indicates that teacher educators paid attention to three main factors as they made decisions about when to pause a candidate: they paid attention to the expertise of the individual candidate who was rehearsing, to the needs of the other participating candidates, and to how many pauses were already occurring in the rehearsal.[4] In some cases, for example, a teacher educator might know of a specific issue on which a candidate had been working; the pauses might focus on that specific issue (in intersection with the focus of the rehearsal, of course). Teacher educators also were constantly attending to how a pause would support not *only* the rehearsing candidate, but also his or her colleagues participating in the rehearsal. In the vignette above, for example, Kevin chose to support Erica in thinking about the ambiguity of her question, not only because Erica herself needed to recognize this, but also because the other participating candidates needed to recognize this ambiguity. Finally, teacher educators weigh how many pauses are appropriate, based on their context. For example, a teacher educator in a residency context might feel comfortable pausing candidates more often than one in a more traditional context, because the educator would know that the candidates were getting regular opportunities to teach K–12 students.

MOVING *BEYOND* A REHEARSAL: DEBRIEFING THE APPROXIMATION
Extending learning past the individual rehearsal

Approximations of practice are designed to provide TCs with opportunities to try out different instructional moves in a low-stakes environment. While likely educative, trying out different moves does not necessarily lead to improved instruction without opportunities for explicit feedback. For comparison, think of a play or musical rehearsal in which the director has two main mechanisms for feedback. The director might pause the actors during a scene to adjust their staging or how lines are delivered. In addition, at the end of the rehearsal, the director provides overarching notes that summarize major areas for growth and establishes goals for future rehearsals. Similarly, in teaching rehearsals, pauses occur throughout the rehearsal but can be supplemented by post-rehearsal debriefs that can extend learning beyond the enactment. The rehearsal debrief presents an opportunity to look at the whole of the practice and chart a path for future professional growth. Whether notes for the actors or debriefing with a TC, post-rehearsal engagement sets the stage for moving the participants toward more effective practice.

The similarities between a play rehearsal and a teaching rehearsal are limited, though. Whereas the director of a play usually provides notes in an expository manner—telling the actors what to change—teaching rehearsal debriefs provide yet another opportunity for inquiry among TCs. The debrief is goal-directed and provides an opportunity for all of the TCs to analyze how students respond to particular moves. However, without structure, rehearsal debriefs can bounce incoherently from one element of practice to another without developing a collective understanding about the practice more broadly. To build collective understanding, we advocate establishing norms (aligned with those in figure 5.1, page 88) amongst the teacher educator and TCs that move away from describing any part of the practice as "good" or "bad." Anecdotally, we have found that debriefs without explicit goals or structure result in a low-level evaluation of practice—"I thought it was really good that you asked that question" or "The way I organized the thoughts on the board was really bad." These types of evaluative statements fall short of helping TCs understand how parts of their practice result in particular student experiences and responses. As noted earlier, when considering planning for the work into a rehearsal, establishing a common purpose for the rehearsal not only supports the actual enactment of the rehearsal (the *through*), but can also frame and support facilitation of the debrief of a rehearsal (the *beyond*), because it provides a clear frame and focus for discussion and reflection for all TCs' learning and development.

One way to avoid an evaluative stance from TCs is to frame the debrief as one in which the community can discuss the cause-and-effect relationship among teaching moves and student responses. For instance, rather than saying a particular question was "good" or "bad," TCs can raise points of the rehearsal in which the teacher asked a particular question or performed a particular move that then resulted in particular forms of responses and actions from the students. Once these teacher-student outcome relationships are identified, the community can inquire into why these relationships exist, and whether these student outcomes are representative of a more generalizable experience.

The debrief can also extend learning beyond the day of the rehearsal. TCs can videotape their rehearsals and, through the use of video annotation tools, reflect on how instructional moves affect student thinking and participation (see vignette below for one example of a reflection assignment). Assigning a video reflection underscores the formative nature of the rehearsal. TCs need in-the-moment feedback as well as opportunities for self-reflection that cannot happen during instruction or even immediately following rehearsal. Rehearsals are stages for both instructional successes and failures, but the value of these experiences is maximized only if opportunities are provided for students to continue inquiring about their practice beyond the boundaries of the rehearsal. Planning a debrief with targeted questions and reflective assignments that narrow the focus to issues of practice has the greatest potential to improve TCs as professionals, not only the rehearsing TC, but all members of the participating community.

Vignette: Continuing the inquiry beyond the rehearsal

Kevin, the science teacher educator described in the above vignette, ended each rehearsal with a seven-minute debrief that was video recorded along with each rehearsal. As the goal of the rehearsal was to allow TCs to practice facilitating a sensemaking discussion about a given data set in the form of a graph, Kevin began the debrief by asking the rehearsing candidate, Erica, "In what ways did your prepared central questions move students toward constructing meaning about a core idea from your given bar graph?"

Erica started by saying, "Oh my gosh, I was so nervous that I know that I said 'Um' about a thousand times." Kevin cut her off and said, "Let's not worry about that—I say the word 'So' when I teach like a thousand times, but it doesn't mean the discussion is ineffective—we all have little nervous tics we need to work on. What about the substance? I mean, think about your questions and what happened when you asked them."

After Erica talked about her central questions and which ones promoted student responses, Kevin opened up the discussion to other members of the class, but focused the talk to two points saying, "Okay, now anyone can jump in—but remember we aren't talking about 'good' or 'bad.' We want to focus just on the use of talk moves to promote uptake of students' ideas or talk about representations—like what was written on the board and why."

After the in-class debrief, each rehearsing TC then continued the cycle of inquiry by completing the following assignment:

Within two days of conducting your rehearsal, reflect on your practice in the following way:

a. *Upload your discussion goals and central questions for the rehearsal in the video annotation software.*
b. *Annotate your video, highlighting a) elements of practice that supported student thinking about the content and b) moves that may have impeded student thinking. In particular, reflect on:*
    i. *the clarity of your framing*
    ii. *the ways in which students were or were not able to take up each others' ideas*
    iii. *the value of representations on the board or projector*
    iv. *the rationale for how you closed the discussion.*
c. *As a final summary annotation at the end of the rehearsal, comment on:*
    i. *one or two specific elements of the practice of leading a sensemaking discussion that should be adapted to further students' thinking*
    ii. *the next instructional task that would continue to move student thinking about the learning goal forward.*

Kevin then used the video annotation software to respond to the TCs' reflections and used some questions that arose as discussion points for the entire class.

MAKING REHEARSALS WORK FOR YOU: PLANNING FOR A REHEARSAL IN YOUR OWN CONTEXT
Making practice public and engaging around it with others
Working collaboratively on practice during rehearsal allows novices to learn not only about ambitious teaching, but also about learning to teach—the

value of making one's teaching public and the benefit in sharing it with others to build a collective understanding of the work. In order to nurture these dispositions, a teacher educator can use a number of practices that include helping novice teachers get in the habit of making practice public, sharing a set of norms for participation in rehearsal, and intervening strategically.

- *Make practice public*: Teaching has long been characterized as a private practice, where teachers are largely isolated from one another in their own classrooms.[5] Rehearsal requires cultivating novices' disposition toward experimenting with teaching in response to student ideas, and toward making their pedagogical practice and reasoning public. This disposition can be nurtured by making safe spaces for novice teachers to propose ideas and try them out with others, and helping them reason about what works (or doesn't) publicly. Engaging TCs in planning activities and then in run-throughs of these activities with each other prior to the rehearsal can support them in developing comfort and a disposition toward making their practice public.

- *Establish norms for participation*: As mentioned earlier in this chapter, it is critical for the success of a rehearsal to establish norms for participation. Being explicit about who does what, when, and for what reasons sets the stage for the kind of public interactions around the work of teaching that will happen during rehearsal. Prior to the very first rehearsal of the course/semester, a teacher educator starts by explaining the participation structure of rehearsal to TCs, describing the roles of the rehearsing teacher, the novices in the audience, and the teacher educator. At this point, teacher educators explain the nature of the feedback they will be giving. They ask TCs who are participating as students to be cooperative in the first few rehearsals so the teacher educator can control the kinds of problems of practice that the rehearsing teacher might grapple with while playing the role of the teacher. It is key for novice teachers not to perceive their first rehearsal as a test of their ability to manage a group of misbehaving students.

- *Intervene strategically*: Establishing and reinforcing a culture of making teaching public also requires supporting TCs in taking risks while experimenting with teaching practices they are not familiar with, and with which they may not always be successful. The teacher educator's interventions—through intentional use of pauses (or the lack of them)—are key in supporting the candidate in taking such risks. In preparing for the rehearsal, determine the sort of problems of practice or the practices that the teacher educator wants to prioritize. The teacher educator's knowledge of the TCs and their teaching experiences (as we will address subsequently) will also inform the teacher educator's interventions and the form of feedback given.

Choosing what to rehearse

A productive rehearsal depends on the selection, study, and flexible use of a teaching event that allows preservice teachers to learn to build lessons around what children can do. For example, in an elementary mathematics classroom, a TC might engage students in choral counting. The teacher leads the class in counting together, deciding, among other things, which number to start with, what to count by (e.g., by 10s, by $\frac{3}{4}$s, etc.), and how to publicly record the count on the board in a manner that affords work on mathematical ideas. TCs can rehearse leading a choral count and learn in the context of this activity how to elicit students' reasoning about patterns and how to represent their thinking to others.

Prior to the start of the rehearsal, it is important for teacher educators to determine what they want the TCs to rehearse and the ideas they want TCs to understand about teaching in the context of a particular instructional activity. Determining the elements of practice that teacher educators want teachers to rehearse shapes how they respond during rehearsal, what they notice about the TC's performance, and what they help TCs notice and understand about teaching.

Additionally, a shared understanding of the general form of the instructional act of focus has been critical to our practice of conducting rehearsals. Both the teacher educator and TCs have in mind the general flow of the lesson, so feedback on instructional decisions is set within this basic structure. To develop such a shared understanding, the teacher educator models the activities in early class sessions. The teacher educator also offers TCs video examples of the activities being enacted with children, and gives them protocols for each activity to support their planning. In leading choral counting, for example, an understanding of the structure of this instructional activity by novices may lead TCs to offer competent introductions, select appropriate and mathematically worthwhile places to stop to elicit students' computational strategies, and elicit student ideas about patterns that emerged in the count. Novices' ability to do this work is a reflection of the aspects of an instructional activity that has become collectively understood and is relatively straightforward to enact. As a consequence, work in rehearsals can then focus on developing a principled elaboration of the activity and on the improvisational decisions that a teacher makes to enact the activity with an appropriate level of rigor and student engagement. The teacher educator uses in-the-moment exchanges in rehearsal to highlight moves that would support a principled enactment of a practice, such as eliciting and responding to student thinking.

Considering the proximity of the rehearsal to enactments with children or youth

What gets worked on in rehearsal is shaped to some extent by how soon the novices will enact the instructional practices with actual children or youth. When rehearsals are nested in cycles that allow novices to enact the instructional practices in actual classrooms, the closeness of these enactments shapes what gets worked on, what TCs pay attention to, and what the teacher educator leverages in his or her feedback.

If the enactment with children or youth is immediately after the rehearsal, there is typically a sense of urgency to focus on aspects of practice that will support successful enactment, such as classroom management, considerations for the kind of errors that may arise, and an intentional focus on what particular students in the teaching context might do. When the enactment is not immediate, it is more typical to talk about various problems of practice more broadly, although TCs might still raise questions related to particular students in their placements.

Adapting the nature of rehearsals over time

As we've noted throughout the sections of this chapter, clearly establishing norms for participation, setting out clear foci within rehearsals, thoughtfully initiating pausing, and publicly debriefing the rehearsal for generative learning, are all important to consider in early instantiations of rehearsing with a group of teachers. As teachers develop their practices and skill sets, the nature of the rehearsals is likely to change, and the teacher educator should consider how to adapt appropriately. As novices work more with students, their ability to anticipate students' responses or possible challenges will arise more often, possibly leading to more pauses initiated by rehearsing or participating TCs. The candidates may bring their own questions to a rehearsal of a particular kind of lesson, requesting a focus for the rehearsal themselves instead of relying on the teacher educator to establish this aspect of the pedagogy. Across our own teacher education contexts, we've found rehearsals to be generative and always changing as TCs grow and develop their practice, and we encourage and welcome these evolutions of the pedagogy as we continue to learn with and from it alongside our TCs.

CLOSING

Rehearsals provide a low-stakes environment for teacher candidates to try particular instructional practices, receive feedback, and gain confidence in their ability to work with both content and students' ideas in a supportive, sheltered setting. Rehearsals are only effective insofar as they are goal-directed, are built on collective norms that move practice beyond evaluation and into an arena of inquiry, and utilize pauses and debriefs in strategic ways that benefit not only the rehearsing teacher candidate, but also the remaining members of the participating community.

Teacher Educator Rehearsal Guidelines for Facilitating Discussion of Visual Texts in Social Studies

OUR GOAL

The goal of our rehearsals on November 16 is to help TCs understand and enact the teaching practice of facilitating a discussion that uses visual texts to develop an understanding of the learning goals and central question.

What to focus on and reasons to pause and rewind during rehearsal, given our purpose:

- Leveled questions and discussion moves are open-ended while also helping students build understanding of learning goals/central question.
  - Pause if questions/moves don't relate to the learning goal or CQ
  - Pause if questions/moves are closed or looking for a right answer, or are leading (it's okay to prompt students to look at specific aspects of the image but do so with open-ended questions, e.g., "What do you notice about the people in this image that might help you think about the CQ?")

- Discussion moves help students return to the texts/images and use details to support reasoning.
  - Pause if there is a missed opportunity to return to the text and support ideas with details, or if attention is being paid to details

that don't help students develop understanding of the learning goals or CQ

- Discussion moves help students listen to, respond to, and build on each other's ideas.
  - Pause if there is a missed opportunity to help students listen, respond to, or build on each other's ideas
  - Pause if the teacher candidate collects student comments without having students consider one idea at a time

- Other reasons for pausing.
  - Wait time: Pause if the teacher candidate fires away with questions without giving people a chance to think and respond
  - Explanations needed: Pause if there seems to be background knowledge that is necessary for students to advance in their thinking; insert explanations judiciously
  - Age appropriateness: Pause if the teacher candidate's enactment does not seem age appropriate.

Issues to discuss during the debrief, given our purpose:
- Content considerations in TCs' materials:
  - Are the learning goals clear?
  - Do the central question and the images support the learning goals? Do these pieces fit together?
  - Is full attribution information included with the documents? It should be (or as much as possible).

- Summarize:
  - Guidance given during the rehearsal.
  - Things the teacher candidate did well.
  - Where there is room for improvement.

STRUCTURE FOR WHAT WILL BE REHEARSED
Each teacher candidate will have twenty minutes (if a group of three) or sixteen minutes (if a group of four) for their rehearsal. Use a timer to

manage time and maintain equity. If there is extra time at the end, go back to unresolved issues. Each teacher candidate's rehearsal will include:

Three or five minutes (three if in a group of four, five if in a group of three)
   (1) Teacher candidate shares background: What are the learning goals, central question, & two images? What details in the image are important for students to notice in order to develop an understanding of the learning goals and CQ?

Nine or ten minutes, including pausing/rewinding
   (2) Teacher candidate teaches by facilitating the last section of his or her discussion in which she or he asks interpretation/ evaluation questions ("Level 3") that compare the images and return to the central question.

Four or five minutes
   (3) Group debrief:
      (1) Give the teaching teacher candidate thirty seconds to an- swer this question: What were you thinking about during that discussion?
      (2) Then ask everyone: What went well? What needs work? [start with positive]

PROTOCOL FOR TEACHER EDUCATORS
During the teacher candidate's rehearsal

- *Affirm*: Look for a reason as soon as possible to publicly affirm the teacher candidate's enactment (e.g., "nice teaching voice or pres- ence"). Share your affirmation audibly while the rehearsal is going on. Must be genuine.
- *Pause and Rewind*: Stop the rehearsal to make a comment, ask a question, or provide a suggestion about some aspect of the prac- tice. Just the teacher educators will do this.
   - *Possible language to use*: "**Let's pause and rewind**," "I no- ticed . . .," "I wondered . . .," "I heard you say . . .," "You

said ____, let's try it again by saying ____ instead," "I see you are annotating by ____, let's try it again by annotating ____."

- *Tone*: We are working together with the teacher candidate so that the practice can be enacted effectively. Remember that the teacher candidates are novices—they don't have your classroom experience. This is hard work for everyone. Avoid a frustrated, judgmental/evaluative, condescending, or impatient tone of voice. Strive for a matter-of-fact tone while still being clear about what to do differently.

• *Redo/Replay*: Have the teacher candidate redo the part that was just discussed and continue on with the rehearsal.

After the teacher candidate's rehearsal

• *Debrief*: Once the teacher candidate is finished rehearsing (and coaching, if time), ask the teacher candidate what he or she was thinking during the discussion—give thirty seconds maximum. Then, ask everyone to give feedback, starting with strengths and then areas for improvement. This is also a time to discuss other issues or points that haven't already come up. Teacher educators should try to summarize key things for the teacher candidate to work on at the end.

Note: Teacher candidates watching will play the role of cooperative students during the rehearsal, to the extent possible. Teacher candidates will participate as themselves during the debrief.

CHAPTER 6

Core Practices and the Teacher Education Curriculum

Stories of Practice

Ashley Cartun, Kristine M. Schutz,
Megan Kelley-Petersen, and Megan Franke

Teacher educators who integrate core practice work into their teacher education programs often approach the integration in one of two ways: (1) at the programmatic level or (2) at the course level. Teacher education programs redesigning their curricula on a programmatic level most often agree upon a common set of core practices they wish to focus on throughout their program, and develop their courses around those practices. Toward this end, teams of teacher educators taking this programmatic approach often launch the effort through collaborative conversations in which they identify and specify a set of practices. For example, as the University of Michigan engaged in the deliberate redesign of their undergraduate program to focus more squarely on practice, teams of faculty, graduate students, and practicing teachers worked together to select and agree upon a set of nineteen practices, which they termed "high-leverage practices," around which they would organize their teacher preparation program.[1] Similarly, the University of Washington structured two of their graduate-level teacher education programs around related sets of core practices that are situated within articulated visions of teaching and learning.

Building from a range of faculty members' work, including intensive field-based methods coursework within the Elementary and Secondary teacher preparation programs, the UW-Accelerated Certification for Teachers (U-ACT) program, and the Seattle Teacher Residency program designed all programmatic coursework to align to each program's set of core practices. Although a challenging process, selecting and specifying practices is just the beginning of the journey to redesigning a program around practice. Once agreed-upon practices are selected, teacher educators pay deliberate attention to how practices are threaded through, addressed, and built upon through the course sequences. Furthermore, redesign committees consider how coursework can allow for deliberate practice of teaching in clinical settings and also adequately incorporate issues of equity and justice into coursework and clinical experiences.

In other instances, teacher educators have begun their work on core practices at the course level and organically build momentum from there. For example, Elizabeth Dutro and Ashley Cartun, faculty at the University of Colorado Boulder, joined the CPC with the intention of integrating core practices into their own writing course and with the hope of expanding this work throughout other courses over time. Similarly, Hala Ghousseini, faculty at the University of Wisconsin, designed her methods course around core practices, and in response to rising interest from her colleagues, created a working group of teacher educators to weave some of these core practices across courses with the hope of building programmatic coherence.

Both of these approaches offer possibilities and challenges, and both require attention to structures, commitments, and engagement over time to create coherence in relation to the core practices. Either form of integration requires attention to the relationship between the core practices, how those practices are engaged with, and how they match the course or program's structures and principled goals. Teacher educators must also pay attention to the experiences of teacher candidates (henceforth TCs) and what it means to understand teaching and learning within and across content, foundations, and field courses. Developing a list of core practices, whether within courses or across the program, is only one aspect of the work of integrating core practices into the teacher education curriculum.

In this chapter, we share our own stories of practice and the ways we each took up work around core practices within our own teacher preparation programs, specifically focusing on how the core practices connected to other program-specific contexts, principles, goals, and commitments. In each of the three stories, the teacher educator situates a suite of core practices within content-specific instructional activities. These instructional activities serve as structures that organize the routines and interactions necessary for responsive teaching. They become rich spaces where novice teachers can not only work on enacting core practices, but also begin to grapple with principles for teaching and develop situated content knowledge for teaching in their respective disciplines.[2] Moreover, each teacher educator incorporates enactment-focused teacher educator pedagogies, such as teacher educator modeling and rehearsal to scaffold candidates' learning.

The stories below examine different grain sizes of our work in order to provide examples of the scope and details that teacher educators might wish to consider when taking up core practices in their programs. Megan Kelley-Petersen's opening story illustrates the use of a learning cycle to highlight how teacher educators and candidates engage in making sense of instructional activities and core practices in her elementary mathematics course. Ashley Cartun's story takes a deeper dive into the way the teacher educator pedagogy of modeling supports TC learning within a Literature as Mentor Text instructional activity. And lastly, Kristine Schutz describes her detailed thinking around the importance of text selection, reading comprehension, and issues of equity in relation to teaching core practices within instructional activities in an early elementary literacy methods course. All of these cases serve to show how instructional activities and core practices are situated in ways that engage the programs' core commitments.

MEGAN KELLEY-PETERSEN'S STORY OF PRACTICE
Setting the Context

As a teacher educator in an accelerated alternative-route certification program, I'm always considering how best to support my novice TCs (who are full-time teachers of record, learning to teach while also teaching full-time) in relevant and ambitious ways. Our program (the U-ACT Program at the University of Washington), uses a framework of core practices as a means for supporting our TCs to both unpack the complexity of teaching practice and to keep it whole and complete. TCs complete coursework across 3 quarters to earn their state residency teaching certificates and can continue on toward a Master's degree if they so choose.

To support the TCs in deepening their teaching practice, I frame their work through instructional activities that help to structure their teaching moves in elementary math. These instructional activities often include multiple core practices, such as eliciting student thinking and orchestrating whole-class discussion. Additionally, we set up the learning experiences for our TCs within a learning cycle (see figure 6.1) so that they're attuned to and aware of how we're thinking strategically about how to consider their contextual needs as full-time teachers and learners.[3] Within

FIGURE 6.1 *Cycle for Collectively Learning to Engage in an Authentic and Ambitious Instructional Activity*

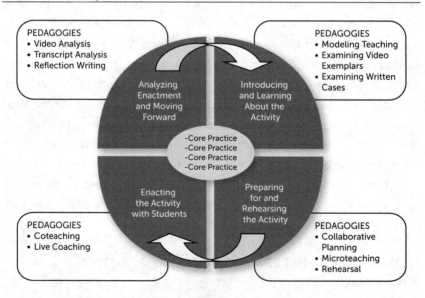

Source: Morva McDonald, Elham Kazemi, and Sarah Schneider Kavanagh, "Core Practices and Pedagogies of Teacher Education: A Call for a Common Language and Collective Activity," *Journal of Teacher Education* 64, no. 5 (2013): 378–386.

the learning cycle, teacher educators lead candidates through a cycle of inquiry in which they first are introduced to an instructional activity and the core practices situated within that activity. Next, candidates prepare to teach the activity and enact the activity with students. And finally, they analyze the enactment and set goals for the next cycle.

Across the entire three-quarter sequence of coursework, the TCs engage in multiple learning cycles around varied instructional activities to develop their teaching around a set of coordinated core practices. While all of these core practices are enacted and "in play" within any instructional activity, I choose to focus novices' attention on only a few core practices at a time. I find that this better supports them to more fully decompose, make sense of, and engage in their development of core practices of teaching. I offer a brief description of each of the core practices as a means to offer an explanation of how we've conceptualized the unpacking of teaching practice in this way. In reality, none of these core practices occur in isolation; in any moment of teaching, a teacher negotiates the interactions between and among students and content. There are multiple instructional decisions and moves that a teacher makes that can fall into any one of these categories, making this framework for decomposing teaching practice incredibly contextual. The cultural and lived experiences of the individual students and the school and classroom community are always necessary to consider and negotiate within these core practices. As a program, U-ACT aspires to a principled perspective and vision of ambitious teaching that challenges inequities, so within any discussion and enactment around these core practices, we're also aiming to attend to issues of equity and justice in striving to build more equitably sustaining classrooms.

Using Core Practices Across a Learning Cycle with an Instructional Activity

I use the instructional activity of *Launch, Explore, Discuss,* drawing heavily on research and resources developed by the field[4] to support TCs' developing understanding of the use of the core practices to teach elementary mathematics. *Launch, Explore, Discuss* an activity that involves coordinating the components of a lesson in a bounded way: 1) posing and *launch*ing a cognitively demanding task to students; 2) monitoring while students work independently or in small groups as they *explore* the content embedded within the task; 3) facilitating a whole-group *discussion* where the teacher has strategically selected and sequenced a few pieces of student work to share.

Within the instructional activity of *Launch, Explore, Discuss*, I support novice TCs in their practice of three of the core practices across the learning cycle: teaching towards instructional goals, positioning students as competent, and orienting students to the content. I hope that by narrowing in on these three, we can work at a deeper understanding and growth of their teaching practice in ways that enable them to attend to the relational work of teaching, the content, and issues of equity. The example here details how I support TCs' development within each of the core practices across the learning cycle within the *Launch, Explore, Discuss* instructional activity.

Quadrant 1: Introducing and learning about the activity I want to position my TCs as competent and support them to see and believe in themselves as mathematicians, so that they, in turn, can foster those same beliefs in their own students. I launch a task, monitor while TCs engage in the mathematical work, and then strategically select and sequence about three pieces of work to facilitate a whole-group discussion. I thoughtfully plan this entire lesson, and after enacting it (with TCs authentically participating as learners), I share my lesson plans with them. This is one example of teacher educator modeling, a representation of practice discussed in chapter 3.

We transition from experiencing the lesson to considering the range of instructional decisions that I made and reflecting on what I had planned to do, on what happened in reality, and on how I may have managed in-the-moment decision making. I justify and rationalize why I chose the pieces of student work to share, and why I shared it in this particular order. I encourage TCs to ask me questions about how I worked to attend to my instructional goal throughout the enactment of the lesson to help them see that, due to the contextual and situational reality of teaching and learning, lessons don't always go as planned. Additionally, I ask TCs to consider how strategically selecting and sequencing students' work to share attends to the core practices of "orienting students to the content" (a teacher only selects a few pieces of work to share, and in a purposeful order to guide the discussion to the key mathematics within the lesson) and "positioning students as competent" (the discussion is entirely framed by the work of the students in the classroom, so they become the experts within the classroom).

After experiencing this kind of a lesson, I create opportunities for TCs to observe elementary-aged students because I want to continue to support them in seeing and believing that all students are capable of rich and rigorous mathematical understanding and discussion. I provide a range of video cases, across grade levels and contexts, so that TCs can watch clips from all components of the lesson structure within classrooms of children closer in age (and context) to their own classrooms. These are also examples of representations of teaching, examined in chapter 2. TCs watch these videos in pairs so that they can discuss specific prompts to support them in reflecting on the varied moves they observe the teachers making in relation to their instructional goals. The prompts push TCs to focus in on the teacher's work to orient students to the content through thinking about the ways that teachers scaffold the content in the lesson, specifically through the strategic selecting and sequencing of student work, and through the supports in launching the lesson. I also orient TCs to consider how the students are positioned throughout the videos: whose knowledge matters, and how? As much as possible, I provide the lesson plans from the teachers in the video(s) so that TCs can reflect on the relationships between the plans and the enactment.

Quadrant 2: Preparing for and rehearsing the activity   As TCs have now engaged in a range of activities to better understand the *Launch, Explore, Discuss* lesson structure, we move into specified planning time for their own classroom contexts. Nearly all assignments in the coursework include lesson planning, videotaped enactments, and reflections from the TCs, so supported and collaborative planning is an important part of the process within class sessions. TCs bring their school/district curricular planning materials with them to the class session and analyze upcoming mathematical tasks to identify a cognitively rich task to pose to their class using a *Launch, Explore, Discuss* lesson structure. TCs consider the cultural and lived experiences of their elementary students and work with teacher educators (and each other) to maintain the mathematical content, but revise the contextual elements of a task to better connect to their students. By carefully considering the context of the task, TCs can better position their students as competent because they're connecting to the range of knowledge and expertise that students bring with them from outside of the formal learning environment of the classroom and school. TCs work to clearly connect the lesson to state standards and to be able to articulate their key instructional goals for the lesson, considering the key mathematical ideas they want highlighted in the various components of the lesson, as well as the key mathematical practices students will engage in across the lesson.

After TCs have had some planning time, I engage them in a rehearsal in order to support them in thinking explicitly about their work within the launch of their lessons. It's much harder to rehearse the latter parts of the lesson given time constraints in our class sessions, so the launch becomes a fruitful moment to consider how to align to our instructional goals and orient students to the content (thinking carefully about what and how to unpack and scaffold in this short discussion before learners set out to work), and how to position students as competent (balancing the high level of cognitive demand of the task while also allowing students to have entry into solving the task on their own or in small groups). Chapter 5 provides a more in-depth discussion on what rehearsals can look like.

Quadrant 3: Enacting the activity with students TCs leave our class session(s) with a solid beginning to their lesson plans for their *Launch, Explore, Discuss* assignment. As they enter their classrooms in the following days, they finalize their lesson plans and enact the lesson with their own students. TCs film their lessons (all three components of the lesson structure) and upload videos and their lesson plans to a secure video platform that the course uses for video sharing. I provide specific prompts that TCs use to complete an accompanying written commentary to individually reflect on their planning and enactment. As seen below, the prompts focus

TCs in on reflecting on the specific core practices worked on within the instructional activity:

1. Summarize your main learning focus: what goal(s) did you have for this specific whole-group discussion?
2. Explain how your understanding of your students' prior academic learning and personal/cultural/community assets guided your instructional choices, both in your choice of the task and in selecting and sequencing your students' ideas to share, in order to develop students' conceptual understanding, mathematical reasoning, and problem- solving skills.
3. Describe and justify why your instructional strategies and planned supports are appropriate for the whole class and for students with similar or specific learning needs. Consider students with IEPs, English language learners, struggling readers, underperforming students or those with gaps in academic knowledge, and/or gifted students.
4. How did you support students to identify resources to support their progress toward the specific goal(s) you had for this whole-group discussion?
5. Describe common mathematical preconceptions, errors, or misunderstandings within your content focus and how you addressed them.

Quadrant 4: Analyzing enactment and moving forward Since we've supported TCs to think critically about specific core practices across the earlier quadrants of the learning cycle, I use specific rubrics to score and provide explicit feedback. We use rubrics from a variety of frameworks that are relevant to our TCs' school/district contexts so that they can align their university coursework with the expectations and formal evaluation systems in their teaching contexts. We primarily use rubrics from the edTPA[5] and the Center for Educational Leadership's Five Dimensions of Teaching and Learning.[6] Our instructional team has considered which rubrics align to which core practices, so I select one rubric for each of the core practices we worked on within *Launch, Explore, Discuss,* and I look for evidence to meet the standards in these rubrics as I read TCs' lesson plans and written commentaries and watch their videos. I provide key action steps for each of the practices to encourage each candidate's growth and development as a teacher. Through other instructional activities, we'll return to each of the core practices multiple times over the course of the academic year, so I aim to provide feedback to TCs that will support this ongoing generative development around core practices.

As I finish scoring TCs' work, we come back together to discuss key themes I noticed across their range of assignments. I often show a few clips from TCs' lessons in a following class session to engage in whole-group discussion to deepen our sense-making around the core practices. Within some assignments, I require TCs to score themselves and reflect on the specific rubrics that I use to consider how self-assessment supports their development and progress.

Reflecting on My Own Learning as a Teacher Educator

As I reflect on experience in my own preparation program (I taught 3rd and 4th grade for multiple years before returning to graduate school myself), I wonder about how much I comprehended about the complexity of teaching practice as a whole while also attending to the in-the-moment instructional decision making. It's hard for me to articulate how/if I had a clear understanding of the varied components and contextual realities of teaching and learning, and the ways to make connections within and across content for my students. I saw myself as an elementary teacher who taught different subjects, and I accordingly changed my instructional practices (and thoughts) for each of these subject areas. It was exhausting, and I knew I needed to learn more to support my practice so that I could better support my amazing students!

While I've by no means solved all of these problems within the design of my coursework around core practices, I'm seeing and hearing TCs in my courses plan, enact, and reflect at a completely different level than I did as a novice teacher. The framework of core practices, in the way that we've envisioned and work to enact them, allows for me to support my TCs in thinking about teaching and learning in a more critical and integrated way. We can simultaneously consider our instructional decisions in relation to content, context, and issues of equity and justice. I continue to strive to create learning opportunities for TCs that empower them to manage this incredibly demanding and rewarding work, and I value the opportunity to continue to refine and reflect on my own practice through collaboration with other teacher educators.

ASHLEY CARTUN'S STORY OF PRACTICE

Setting the Context

As teacher educators working within an undergraduate elementary teacher licensure program at CU Boulder, Elizabeth Dutro and I were interested in more explicitly addressing the core practice of "modeling" in our writing methods course. It is important to note that modeling is not only a core practice but it is also an essential pedagogy of enactment for teacher educators. We were already using four instructional activities to structure TCs' practice, but wanted to make our thinking more transparent when it came to the kinds of decisions that went into developing minilessons for Writer's Workshop. In what follows, I share my story about choosing one instructional activity, Using Literature as Mentor Text, and my process of developing a minilesson with the Core Practice Consortium resources on modeling as my guide.

Embedded on-site methods course   Our writing methods course was designed to support undergraduates in the first semester of their teacher license program.[7] The course draws heavily on the Writer's Workshop method to teach writing content in a practice-based, embedded course setting in which both the university course content and practicum components occur together at our long-standing partnership school, Franklin Elementary, a Title I elementary school within the Denver metro area. We teacher educators (teaching the course) and TCs meet weekly at the school for a full day and partner closely with a third-grade teacher (and developing teacher educator), Alex, and her whole class of third-grade students.

The course uses instructional activities to structure TC learning with four different kinds of minilessons during Writer's Workshop: 1) modeled writing, 2) using literature as a mentor text, 3) conferencing, and 4) interactive writing (in that order). The TCs use these four instructional activities to progress through an instructional cycle, planning, rehearsing, enacting and debriefing their four distinct lesson plans that they enact with their third-grade "buddies" during the semester. Each instructional activity was designed to support the learning occurring in Alex's classroom and encourages TCs' engagement with equity-oriented lessons and pedagogies.

The weekly structure of our full day together begins with the undergraduates arriving to the school in the morning and meeting in Franklin's common "pod" area to have our university-based content methods course. The TCs then break up into teaching teams and use the learning cycle to rehearse their lesson plans for one of the instructional activities, with us circulating to provide feedback and support. After lunch, the TCs enact their lessons with their third graders that very same day.

For each new instructional activity, we progress through a scaffolded approach that introduces the instructional activity during the morning methods class session, followed by several opportunities to watch the instructional activity in action, which includes getting to observe Alex and one of us (teacher educators) modeling the instructional activity or practice. The TCs then begin the learning cycle by developing lesson plans using the instructional activity, rehearsing the instructional activity (with their lesson plans), enacting it with their third-grade students, and finally debriefing the lesson with peers and teacher educators.

Guiding program commitments and principles   Our elementary teacher education program is guided by a series of connected principles that frame every aspect of our work in schools and with TCs: 1) teachers must position students as sense-makers and knowledge-generators; 2) teaching is both intellectual work and a craft; 3) teachers must design equitable learning environments in which all children are engaged in robust and consequential learning; and 4) teachers' instruction and student learning is always conducted within the context of larger social systems, structures, and hierarchies.

Our writing course was designed around the premise that candidates need concrete opportunities to observe and enact social justice and equity-oriented philosophies, curricula and pedagogies. The instructional activities taken up in the course provide space to use writing and texts that push on dominant narratives and provide more diverse and expansive bodies, ideas, and ways of being.

Focusing on The Core Practice of Modeling Using Literature as a Mentor Text

Supporting TCs' understandings of instructional activities Although Elizabeth and I had designed this course as an instructional activity in Writer's Workshop in the spring of 2013, we wanted to make the core practice of modeling even more explicit when students observed our enactments of using a piece of literature as a mentor text. To do this, I returned to the CPC description of modeling as a guiding resource to be sure I used the elements of modeling and embedded them into my minilesson. Learning how to mine a mentor text with children is a complex practice; my goal in using the core practice of modeling as a guide was to highlight my own thinking as a teacher and to bring attention to certain moves that I make when I use a piece of writing as a learning tool for my own writing.

Prior to the minilesson For this instructional activity, the TCs had the opportunity to observe their mentor teacher, Alex, enact this kind of lesson during Writer's Workshop with the third graders, followed by my modeling of a Literature as Mentor Text (LMT) minilesson during class time. My lesson would then transition TCs into developing their own LMT lesson plans for Writer's Workshop. These are two different, but related, representations of teaching.

Planning my lesson for TCs I developed my minilesson in order to demonstrate one way to use a mentor text in Writer's Workshop, to model the core practice of modeling for students during a lesson, and to use a text that supported social-justice philosophies without it being the central focus of the lesson. I also wanted to demonstrate how teachers might use a fictional text, in this case a children's picture book, to focus in on a particular element of writing that their third graders could use as a tool to enhance their own personal narratives.

I selected my LMT minilesson objectives based on the elements of writing that I knew our third-grade buddies were currently working on as part of a personal narrative unit. In this minilesson, I focused on how the author helped the reader to visualize the text, and how a simile can be one tool to help readers paint a picture in their minds. I used the children's book *Stand Tall, Molly Lou Melon* in the modeled minilesson. The book, often found on feminist reading lists, features Molly Lou, a young girl who remains confident and proud of her non-normative body with the help of her encouraging grandmother. This text was selected because of its underlying message, but also for the ways in which the author uses figurative language, like similes, to help the readers visualize the text. As highlighted in the lesson plan document in table 6.1, I revisited the CPC's definition of modeling to ensure that I highlighted those aspects of modeling during my minilesson with TCs. Before enacting the minilesson, I made sure that my TCs had been introduced to the core practice of modeling and to the CPC's definition and indicators of the practice. The TCs were to play the role of third graders, and I took on the role of their teacher during Writer's Workshop. For the sake of the modeled lesson, we were going to pretend that we had experienced previous minilessons where I had introduced both the goal of helping readers visualize the text and the literary element of similes.

After watching my minilesson, TCs got the opportunity to develop their own LMT lessons using a preselected common text, *A Chair for My Mother*. We chose this text because it was a story that aligned with equity-oriented goals and lent itself to similar learning objectives as my modeled minilesson. *A Chair for My Mother* tells the story of Rosa, a young girl whose family (a daughter, mother and grandmother) lose their possessions in a house fire. Rosa wants to buy her mother a comfortable chair she can relax in after a long day working as a waitress. Although it takes some time, the family is able to save enough coins to buy a new chair, bringing joy to everyone.

Decomposing practice with TCs   After I taught my minilesson with my TCs, I paused the lesson to step out of our roles (me as teacher and the TCs as the third graders) to decompose the practice of modeling. I transitioned by saying, "I'm going to stop there. Let's think about my minilesson as an example of modeling Literature as Mentor Text. What do you find yourself noticing about what I modeled? What did you notice I was doing?"

TABLE 6.1 *Teacher Educator Planning Notes for Enacting the Modeled Lesson: from CPC Specification of Modeling*

DEFINITION OF MODELING (SPRING 2015)	*The practice of making one's own thinking visible while using a process, strategy, or technique within the discipline in order to make accessible to students the thinking, decision making and actions that are critical to the work.*	
COMPONENT OF MODELING	**INDICATORS**	**ASHLEY'S MINILESSON SCRIPT ENACTING THE COMPONENTS OF PRACTICE**
Framing the work	• Connects the current lesson to students' ongoing learning. • Tells students what they are going to learn in this lesson (e.g., states intent to model how to ____, tells students that the teacher is going to show them how to ____). • Provides and explains the purpose of using a particular strategy or technique to achieve an identified goal (i.e., what and how).	Writers, since we've been thinking about personal narratives, we've talked about lots of tools we can use to bring our stories to life. Just like we've discussed in earlier lessons, using tools like a hook to draw the reader in and organizing our personal narratives using a strong beginning, middle, and end can be really powerful. So today, I would like for us to think of another tool that we as writers can use to bring our story to life, and that is *visualizing the text*. And just like we have seen in other stories, visualizing the text is where the author's words paint a clear picture in our minds. So today, I am going to read just a few pages of a fictional story to you that I love. It is called *Stand Tall, Molly Lou Melon* by Patty Lovell. While this book is a picture book and has beautiful illustrations, what I am most interested in is that even if I just read the words without the pictures, I am able to picture images in my mind. Our purpose today is to ask ourselves what the author does to help us readers visualize the text.

continues

TABLE 6.1 *Continued*

DEFINITION OF MODELING (SPRING 2015)	*The practice of making one's own thinking visible while using a process, strategy, or technique within the discipline in order to make accessible to students the thinking, decision making and actions that are critical to the work.*	
COMPONENT OF MODELING	INDICATORS	ASHLEY'S MINILESSON SCRIPT ENACTING THE COMPONENTS OF PRACTICE
Making thinking, decision making, and action used in applying the strategy visible	• Accurately demonstrates one way of using the targeted strategy or technique. • Thinks aloud about and/or dramatizes key elements of the work. • Avoids attending to nonessential aspects of the process, strategy, or technique (e.g., avoids rambling, avoids sharing distracting details).	So, listen while I explain what I'm thinking about as a writer when I read the first few pages of this text. I want you to watch how I focus in on using the writer's craft of *simile* to help me write a personal narrative that lets the author visualize the text. As a writer, I'm noticing how Patty Lovell is including similes to help her readers visualize the text. Using a simile might be one thing I may want to try out to help my readers visualize a text. [Read first five pages and stop on the fifth page.] Wow. I had so many pictures come into my mind when I read that page. I can picture a big, old bullfrog with a mean snake squeezing it, making the frog make a horrible noise. I can even hear the noise in my mind! I can picture this sound coming from Molly Lou singing really loud so everyone can hear her. Pay attention to what I do as a writer. As a writer, I want to look at this page and see what the author did that made me picture Molly Lou and her singing voice so clearly. Read the first line again: "Molly Lou Melon had a voice that sounded like a bullfrog being squeezed by a boa constrictor."

COMPONENT OF MODELING	INDICATORS	ASHLEY'S MINILESSON SCRIPT ENACTING THE COMPONENTS OF PRACTICE
Highlighting the aspects of the work that are key and can be transferred to other situations	• Articulates a clear sequence in the process of using the strategy or technique. • Concisely shares reasoning process involved in engaging in a particular task (e.g., "I know narratives include many details. For this reason, I am going to write . . ."). • Uses verbal markers to draw students' attention to areas of the work that are particularly important or challenging (e.g., "Pay close attention as I . . ." "Did you see how I . . ."). • Avoids attending to nonessential aspects of the process, strategy, or technique (e.g., avoids rambling, avoids sharing distracting details)	Did you notice how I just reread that sentence? As I reread the sentence, I recognize something I have seen before in other stories. The author used a simile to help us picture and even hear Molly Lou Melon's unique singing voice! I really like the way the author uses a simile here to help me visualize the text. As a writer, I'm saying to myself, I think I am going to try using a simile in visualizing my personal narrative.

I asked the candidates to reference their handouts on modeling to guide our discussion. After TCs shared several noticings about the minilesson, I introduced the LMT lesson plan template that they would use to design their own lessons. I tried to make sure they saw the connection between the instructional activity and the previous experiences they have had with modeling. "So, again, thinking about one of our core practices, modeling, you'll see places in this lesson template where you are encouraged to build in some of those modeling moments."

Teacher Candidate Take-Up of Modeling

The scaffolded lesson plan guided the TCs in designing a lesson for their third graders around the goal of noticing how an author stretches a small moment in a narrative to create an interesting story by using descriptive details. In addition to learning goals for each instructional activity lesson plan, TCs also developed an equity goal, in which they explicitly identified a goal for noticing children and positioning all students as knowledge generators. They also identified ways in which they intended to analyze their language and interactions in their lesson debriefs.

The LMT lesson plan template had certain sections already developed (which became less scaffolded as the semester continued). For example, the "preparing for instruction" section of the LMT lesson plan made some of the lesson rationale clearer to TCs. It read, "choose an engaging picture book that focuses on a personal narrative that fosters, connection for students. For this lesson, we'll all use *A Chair for My Mother*, by Vera B. Williams. Become familiar with the book—read it through a time or two. Then, read it specifically to locate points in the text where you will stop to notice how the author uses description and vivid language to expand a small moment within the story."

As TCs progress through their lessons, they use sentence starters and phrases that resemble the kinds of modeling they encountered when I modeled the minilesson.

Reflecting on My Own Learning as a Teacher Educator

In reflecting on my lesson development, I found it to be incredibly helpful to use the CPC's document on modeling. I wanted to be sure I was clear on and familiar with the components of modeling and bring those components to the TC's attention in the context of an instructional activity that they would be developing on their own. By using modeling as a key guide in a lesson I regularly used in my course, I felt like I was able to further enhance a practice that was already meaningful and aligned with our course's goals and my personal and programmatic commitments around social justice.

KRISTINE SCHUTZ'S STORY OF PRACTICE
Setting the Context

At the University of Illinois at Chicago (UIC), I teach literacy methods courses in our undergraduate urban elementary education program. The program is organized around a decolonizing framework for teacher preparation that aims to complexify our definition of high-quality teaching, and equip novice teachers with the knowledge, skills, and mindsets to disrupt the status quo and create anti-racist and socially-just spaces for learning.[8] Surrounded by some of the most critically-oriented faculty colleagues in the country, I have begun to take a more critical stance as a teacher educator and push my practice in ways that attend to issues of injustice and oppression in our nation. I teach two literacy methods courses to an undergraduate cohort across the fall and spring semesters. The first course occurs during candidates' first semester in the teacher education program and addresses early literacy content with a focus on print literacies. Within the course, we also devote time to developing a working definition of literacy/ies and exploring language ideologies. Wrestling with these ideas early on seems particularly important given that the majority of our candidates are preparing to teach in urban schools. In the spring, the second course addresses literacy instruction and assessment in upper elementary classrooms.

The Use of Instructional Activities

I design my courses around a suite of instructional activities and assessment activities with the goal of preparing candidates to enact ambitious, culturally-relevant literacy instruction. Understanding text comprehension, how it occurs, and what teachers can do to support and improve children's comprehension is an important focus across the year. I strive to help candidates understand the complexity of text comprehension and that it is the intersection of multiple factors—the text, activity, sociocultural context, and the reader—that impacts comprehension, not just the readers themselves.[9] Across the courses, I use three instructional activities to situate candidates' learning about text comprehension: interactive read-aloud, think-aloud assessment, and text-based discussion. The activities not only serve as structures for organizing instruction and assessment, but also as spaces for attending to core practices that candidates can transfer to their teaching of mathematics, science, and social studies. The suite of instructional activities connects to our work on text comprehension, and within the activities I focus on three core practices over time: (1) establishing a learning environment, (2) facilitating discussion, and (3) eliciting and responding to student thinking.

To support candidates in learning to enact the activities, I incorporate the use of a learning cycle[10] to provide candidates with coordinated experiences viewing and unpacking representations of the instructional or assessment activity, preparing for instruction, teaching in their field placements, and analyzing instruction. However, unlike many applications of the learning cycle discussed in this book, contextual factors, such as the structure of field placements, often limit candidates' ability to iterate. In other words, candidates often enact the instructional activity with children only once during the course. I encourage candidates to capitalize on informal opportunities to work with instructional and assessment activities in the field. While this is not ideal, it still provides candidates with opportunities to enact and analyze teaching.

Interspersed within the learning cycle are other opportunities for candidates to engage in equity-oriented experiences and conversations. For example, prior to learning about any instructional activities, the class reads the text, *Other People's Words: The Cycle of Low Literacy,*[11] and together we puzzle about how to define literacy/ies. These experiences help candidates begin to develop an understanding of literacy/ies as a social practice, the mismatch between home and school literacies, and the need for culturally-sustaining[12] literacy teaching.

Text selection for instructional activities   As I've become more aware of the nuance of the representation of people from traditionally marginalized groups in texts and seen the power of disruption through counternarratives, text selection has become an even more critical aspect of course design. I strive to expose candidates to high-quality and culturally relevant texts that they can use in future teaching. Although I had historically identified texts that enabled children to see themselves reflected in texts and helped candidates to analyze and select culturally relevant text sets, I now incorporate the use of intentionally selected texts that attend to equity concepts for teaching. I use these texts to expand candidates thinking about what justice-oriented literacy instruction entails. In addition, these same texts are used to support candidates in enacting instructional activities and core practices.

In the first literacy methods course, I use four children's books as we learn to enact interactive read-alouds. On the first day of class, I model a read-aloud using the book *Red: A Crayon's Story* by Michael Hall.[13] This is a story about a crayon named Red, that has a red label even though he is blue. His family, teacher, and friends do everything they can to help him act like a red crayon, but no matter how hard he tries, he cannot do it. One day, Red meets another crayon named Berry. Berry offers a new perspective that enables Red to discover Red's true self, that is, blue. I read the story using the structure for the interactive read-aloud that candidates will later learn, and I focus on helping candidates understand the power of Berry's counternarrative. Through discussion, we explore the impact of implicit and explicit messages about identity and competence. After modeling, I extend the discussion to help candidates relate our conversation about the ideas in the text to teaching and children. Although candidates will not be formally introduced to interactive read-alouds for a few weeks, this common experience helps us begin to develop a common vision of interactive read-alouds and connects with equity-oriented concepts.[14] Although there is no discussion of core practices when reading this text, I deliberately model the three core practices listed above within the interactive read-aloud.

For our second interaction with a children's text, we use the book *The Other Side* by Jaqueline Woodson.[15] In this text, Woodson tells the story of an African American child and a white child who live on opposite sides of the fence and are warned not to go to the other side. Woodson chronicles the development of the two girls' friendship and the way in which they dismiss segregating rules and viewpoints. Before turning to the text, I introduce candidates to a structure for interactive read-aloud text introductions. I accomplish this through an inquiry process in which the class views and compares two videos of teachers enacting text introductions to co-construct a list of features of supportive text introductions. By sharing contrasting examples of text introductions, candidates see and identify teacher moves that activate and prime relevant prior knowledge to support comprehension, and we begin to decompose the core practice of establishing a learning environment. For homework, candidates then read and analyze the text and draft a text introduction based on the features we identified.

The following week in class, we engage in our first rehearsals of text introductions. Because the purpose of the early rehearsals is to build community and trust so candidates feel comfortable taking risks and being vulnerable in their developing practice, I mainly attend to the practice of establishing a learning environment as I coach the rehearsals. For example, I might draw attention to using inclusive language within the introduction. Each time I use this text with candidates, someone always raises the question of the appropriateness of using a text that talks about such "meaty" or "sophisticated" topics. I intentionally devote time in class to discussing this, helping candidates come to understand that it is our obligation as educators to engage children in conversations about race, bias, privilege, and oppression. We begin to brainstorm possible ways into these conversations, and we continue this work throughout the semester.

In preparation for the following class, candidates read the text *Yesterday I Had the Blues* by Jeron Ashford Frame.[16] *Yesterday I Had the Blues* is a lyrical text in which an African American boy tells the tale of different moods he and his family members experience over time, using colors to represent different moods. The rich and detailed illustrations enhance the story, helping readers understand why the characters are experiencing particular moods. The story closes with the boy emphasizing that in spite of all the changing moods, everything is "all golden" in his family. I use this text for a number of reasons. First, it allows many of the students the candidates will teach to see and hear themselves in the story. Second, it provides a counternarrative to a dominant social narrative that might be held by some candidates in the course and children in the classes they teach. We discuss these ideas and my thinking behind the text selection, and then connect this conversation to what candidates are learning about language, dialect, and register.

We use *Yesterday I Had the Blues* as a common text that all candidates will use when enacting their first interactive read-alouds in their classrooms. I incorporate multiple levels of support to help candidates prepare for the enactment and learn inside the preparation. First, we watch a video of a former candidate, Nicole, facilitating a read-aloud of the text with a group of first graders. The structure and routines of the instructional activity and her enactment of the core practices of focus—establishing a learning environment, eliciting student thinking, facilitating discussion, and providing instructional explanations—are consistent with the vision of practice that I share with candidates. I use this video for a number of reasons. First, viewing a novice as opposed to an expert teacher helps candidates envision themselves doing the same sort of work with children. Second, because Nicole was at a similar place in her program when she taught the lesson, the structure of the routines and the ways in which she enacts the practices appear more punctuated. In other words, the components of the interactive read-aloud and ways of enacting practices that candidates are working on appear more clunky than that of a seasoned teacher whose instruction is more fluid by virtue of experience. Finally, I hypothesize that using a video that aligns with the plan and vision of practice I hold reduces cognitive load for candidates as they do not need to make sense of conflicting messages about teaching practice. After viewing and debriefing the video, we analyze the plan that Nicole used and modify any sections that we agree need to be changed before we settle on a common lesson plan. It is important to note that candidates can modify some aspects of the plan on their own, but they need to be able to articulate their decision making. Few TCs choose to change much at this place in their development. We then continue to proceed through the learning cycle and prepare for teaching by rehearsing the interactive read-aloud.

During the rehearsals, I draw attention to the focal core practices and support candidates in learning to enact them. I also work to bolster candidates' specialized content knowledge for teaching reading inside the rehearsals. For example, we discuss what an inference is, and in the case of this text, we consider how to support children to make inferences by paying close attention to the illustrations and connecting them to what the text is saying. Multiple candidates rehearse, and we continue constructing a collective understanding of shared practice. Candidates then teach this lesson in their field placements and analyze their teaching for places in which they enacted the core practices.

Our final activity in the first methods course that is specific to interactive read-alouds and text comprehension uses the text *My Best Friend* by Mary Ann Rodman.[17] In this text, Lily narrates a story about a summer in which she tried to befriend an older girl named Tamika. In spite of all Lily's attempts, Tamika mistreats her. In the end, Lily ends up befriending another girl at the pool who exhibits care and interest in their friendship. I select this text for a number of reasons. First, it is a humanizing representation of black youth. Second, the text is written in a way that requires readers to make a number of high-level inferences to understand how Tamika's actions impact Lily. This enables us to work on the core practice of providing instructional explanations, specifically modeling how to make inferences and support children in making inferences. Modeling is a particularly difficult practice for candidates to enact as it requires them to not only demonstrate a strategy, skill, or process, but also to annotate their thinking in order to decompose the process and give children access to their decision making. Modeling in reading poses another challenge, as teachers must think aloud to give children access to their process while demonstrating.[18]

I launch the work with *My Best Friend* by having candidates read and identify potential instructional goals for the interactive read-aloud. The class then collaboratively identifies instructional goals, one of which is making inferences by paying close attention to what characters say and do to understand how they are feeling. I then share a draft of the text introduction, and the candidates coplan the "during and after reading" parts of the read-aloud, including moments in which they will model inferring and guide children through using this strategy, as well as the questions they will use to initiate discussion about the ideas in the text. As with the previous read-aloud, we rehearse parts of the lesson, focusing mainly on the parts of the plan that candidates drafted. During the rehearsals, I attend mainly to aspects of the focal core practices—facilitating discussion and providing instructional explanations (modeling). Although I encourage novices to enact this lesson in their field placements, not all of them can, so I rely on the in-class experience of planning and approximating teaching to support their growth.

Reflecting on My Own Learning as a Teacher Educator

In reflecting on my own experience modifying my course to begin to more adequately ensure equity in literacy education, I know that this is just a small step. I remain committed to using both core practices and instructional activities to help candidates learn to do the actual work of teaching. To me, it is an issue of equity that unprepared teachers are placed in the classrooms of our most vulnerable populations. I see practice-based teacher education as way of ensuring that new teachers are ready to hit the ground running on their first days in classrooms and provide all children, but especially those from traditionally marginalized populations, the kind of instruction, love, and respect they deserve. My early experiences at UIC, however, have taught me that this is not enough. What I once thought was socially-just teaching really wasn't. And the story of practice I've shared is just the start of my journey to discover what it does mean to prepare candidates, in real and practical ways, to disrupt and transform.

THE RELATIONAL NATURE OF CORE PRACTICES: IMPLICATIONS FOR DESIGNING TEACHER EDUCATION CURRICULUM

These stories from Megan, Ashley, and Kristine highlight the complexities of learning to teach in a way that is responsive to students, content, our respective contexts, and the broader sociopolitical context. The stories demonstrate how the manner in which core practices are integrated into the curriculum is strongly influenced by programmatic goals and commitments and by the structures that shape the work. Each story provides a close look at the teacher educator's decision making as they design coursework around core practices situated within content-specific instructional activities. Moreover, they serve as examples of how teacher educators enact pedagogies such as modeling and rehearsal to provide and create images of the kinds of ambitious instruction they wish for their TCs to enact with children.

In our view, core practice work is both situational and relational; using core practices and instructional activities is less about simply identifying core practices and more about reimagining teacher education practice in ways that acknowledge and take advantage of the relational and situated nature of teaching and learning. For us, this means that there isn't a single set of correct core practices. Our work, and what is core to the field of teaching, will always bend and flex to the needs of students in response to the greater social systems that impact schools. Our stories also make clear that the work is not just about carefully defining the core practices individually. Rather, it is about how the core practices are used in relation *to each other* to support learning, and how those core practices are used within an activity to meet the needs of learners.

Using core practices to center one's teacher education practice is a collective activity. It is collective in terms of how we work within our classroom spaces with our students; it is collective in how we work across elements of our programs; it is collective in how we consider the communities in which we teach and learn. Our core practices serve as a tool for ongoing negotiation about what we value and what we know about what can support candidates' learning to teach.

The stories told here demonstrate the kinds of negotiations we each made within our particular spaces and in relation to our commitments. Although each teacher preparation program differs in context and the students they support, all three stories demonstrate how core practices can challenge inequities when situated in relevant content and guided by equity-oriented program principles.

There is a clear need as teacher educators to discuss and articulate our reasons for why we do what we do. Our current sociopolitical context makes it more critical than ever for teacher educators, TCs, and educators in the field to engage in robust conversations about our commitments and how we enact those commitments in our practice, and to create spaces for our learners to do the same. Core practice work supports efforts to disrupt the status quo in public schools and "help novice teachers counter long-standing inequities in the schooling experiences of children, particularly youth from communities that continue to be marginalized in the US."[19] Driven by these commitments, core practices can serve as resources and tools to support equity-minded instruction within teacher preparation programs and K–12 school settings.

CHAPTER 7

Taking Core Practices to the Field

Andrea Bien, Janet Carlson, Elham Kazemi,
Abby Reisman, Melissa A. Scheve, and Andrea Wells

The preceding chapters lay out a new vision for teacher education, one that transforms university-based methods courses into sites that tackle the intricacies and contingencies of practice. Our goal has been to illustrate teacher education pedagogies that deliberately blur the line between theory and practice. At the same time, we recognize that if we truly wish to dismantle the rigid conceptual divide between theory and practice, we must leave the university campus. In this chapter, we explore ways we might bring teacher education around core practices to the field. We understand the field to be K–12 classrooms in actual schools where both preservice and in-service teachers work. We describe examples of programs and projects that have taken practice-based teacher education beyond the university classroom, and we suggest structural and institutional reforms that would further support such work across a teacher's development and career.

WHY LEAVE THE UNIVERSITY CLASSROOM?

For core practice work to succeed, it needs to be responsive to the demands and realities of school settings. We see three clear reasons why we need to take this work beyond the university classroom. First, in the context of preservice teacher education, it should be evident that the closer to the field one can be when learning about and attempting to enact core practices, the richer the learning will be. The issue in the case of preservice teacher education is structural and infrastructural, as moving beyond the university classroom requires reimagining how schools can serve as sites for novice learning.

The second reason that core practice work must attend to the demands of the field is that it must consider teachers' ongoing learning and development beyond their preparation and certification programs. The literature on teacher learning shows that professional growth and development continue long after preservice education ends. Practice-based support for in-service teachers must serve the needs of both teachers who have engaged in practice-based learning in their preservice programs, as well as in-service teachers who have not yet engaged in professional learning focused on core practices.

Finally, and relatedly, without attending to the demands and realities of the field, we risk perpetuating existing structures of inequity. It is important to underscore that an emphasis on core practices is an emphasis on those instructional activities that elevate students' voices, encourage active participation, and initiate students into processes of inquiry and knowledge construction in ways that counter longstanding inequities, particularly for children and youth from marginalized communities.

Below, we organize our discussion of field-based supports for practice-based teacher education into two broad categories. First, we take a close look at what it might mean to design and support field-based mentoring and coaching around core practices for both preservice and in-service teachers; second, we make an argument for longer-term models of teacher learning that support teacher development through induction and early-career stages. We illustrate these ideas with examples drawn from a variety of contexts in which we have engaged in teaching core practices, including a teacher residency program; a university-based methods class that incorporates time in classrooms; a two-year professional development program that combines both face-to-face experiences and analysis of classroom videos to develop early-career teachers' use of core practices; and a job-embedded model of teacher professional learning that takes place in classrooms and schools.

MENTORING AND COACHING TEACHERS IN CORE PRACTICES

One of the first places we might look as we move beyond the university classroom is how to support mentors who work with preservice teachers, and coaches who provide ongoing support to in-service teachers. Below we discuss two programs that have taken strides to better understand and support these essential roles.

Boston Teacher Residency: Supporting Classroom Mentors

Boston Teacher Residency (BTR) is the site of our first example of a program striving to bring core practices to in-service teachers working in the field. At the time that we studied the program, BTR placed preservice teachers, called residents, in the classrooms of experienced mentor teachers, or collaborating teachers, in a Boston Public Schools partner school. The residents received extensive guidance on their planning and teaching from the collaborating teacher as well as from BTR clinical teacher educators, who taught residents' coursework and coached them on their teaching. The clinical teacher educators worked in the field with residents in their school placements each day, teaching degree-required methods coursework and coaching them individually, in pairs, and as a group. Importantly, the clinical teacher educator also supported the collaborating teachers in their roles, an illustration of taking core practices to the field that will be elaborated below. Additionally, following graduation, residents received three years of induction support from BTR, which took the form of individual or small-group coaching by a BTR faculty or staff member.

The core practice of whole-class discussion in BTR   BTR has a strong social-justice orientation. The program actively recruits residents of color, and the majority of students in the schools in which residents are placed receive free or reduced lunch. The program also articulates goals for teaching and learning that promote equity, which, at the time of the study, included a focus on the core practice of whole-class discussion; content-focused, whole-class discussion was seen as a way to give K–12 students an opportunity to make sense of important content ideas, and as a way to promote equity by keeping student reasoning and student voices at the center.

BTR residents learned to plan and teach cognitively demanding lessons, treat students as sense-makers, and maintain a consistent focus on student reasoning for all students. They also learned foundational principles for "building a productive learning environment where every student matters and participates." Before graduating, all residents were required to pass performance assessments in planning and teaching, and the corresponding lesson that the residents taught included a required component of whole-class discussion.

Residents learned the practice of facilitating a whole-class discussion incrementally over the course of the residency. Clinical teacher educators modeled content-focused whole-class discussions in content lessons starting the summer before school started and continuing into the school year. Residents planned for discussions in their placement classrooms with extensive support, through content methods classes, small group planning sessions, and one-on-one coaching. In content methods classes, residents rehearsed the discussions they would facilitate with their students. When they led discussions in their classrooms, they often received in-the-moment coaching from the clinical teacher educator and the collaborating teacher. Debrief sessions followed, with both the clinical teacher educator and the collaborating teacher present, and the group analyzed low-inference notes, student work, and/or video as they considered what students seemed to understand, and then planned the next steps for resident and student learning. Key to the success of this work was BTR's support for the collaborating teachers who supported the residents as they learned to enact this core practice.

Support for collaborating teachers   A significant part of the clinical teacher educator's work was to support the collaborating teachers in their mentoring of the residents, and to facilitate the relationship between the collaborating teacher and the resident. While collaborating teachers were all experienced teachers, they brought a variety of strengths and viewpoints. They may or may not have been graduates of BTR. They may have had varying degrees of comfort facilitating whole-class discussions themselves, as this is a challenging practice for most teachers, and is often not taught in teacher preparation programs. In fact, the collaborating teacher may have felt ambivalent about the value of whole-class discussion, having struggled with it or seen it go awry in the past. Thus, the clinical teacher educator built on the collaborating teachers' strengths and supported the collaborating teachers in allowing the residents to try practices that they may not have felt fully comfortable with. The clinical teacher educator also supported each collaborating teacher's ongoing coaching of the residents in this practice, as the collaborating teachers were in the classroom with the residents every day, while the clinical teacher educator was not. This was challenging, given that preservice teachers often did not, at first, implement the practice with a great deal of success, which can contribute to ambivalence on the part of a collaborating teacher about the value of discussion. So the clinical teacher educator had to work to help the collaborating teachers see the value of whole-class discussion, and had to encourage them to support the residents' attempts at the practice. Finally, to the extent possible, the clinical teacher educator worked with the collaborating teachers in implementing the practice of whole-class discussion in their own teaching. In many cases, the collaborating teacher did value whole-class discussion, and was enthusiastic about the coaching received as part of the relationship with BTR. Regardless, collaborating teachers found their participation in the program to be valuable for their practice as mentors to residents as well as teachers of K–12 students.

While BTR also supports in-service teachers with induction support for graduates of the program, here we focus specifically on support the program offered to the collaborating teachers in work related to the core practice of whole-class discussion. This support took a variety of forms, both formal and informal. The clinical teacher educator led monthly professional learning opportunities for the collaborating teachers, which were focused on both supporting their residents and honing their own teaching practice. These professional learning activities were often related to the core practice of whole-class discussion and were informed by the clinical teacher educator's insider knowledge of the residents' and collaborating teachers' struggles and successes with the practice. In these sessions, the clinical teacher educator might, for example, have chosen to show classroom video of a teacher successfully facilitating a whole-class discussion, then engaged the collaborating teachers in a conversation about moves the teacher made that resulted in students explaining their thinking or students responding to each other's ideas—skills that the residents were learning. Collaborating teachers might then reflect on the extent to which their residents were doing the specific things seen in the video, and consider ways in which they could support their residents in this work— including modeling the practice themselves.

Another way the clinical teacher educator might use video in monthly professional learning sessions was to choose a technique that residents were working on, and many were struggling with, for example, a *turn and talk*. Residents learned this technique as a way to support all students in engaging in the practice of whole-class discussion. The clinical teacher educator might show short clips of several residents attempting a turn and talk, and the group might reflect on the strengths of each approach and discuss ways they might coach each resident. This allowed collaborating teachers to see examples of the technique being implemented with varying degrees of success, and gave the group an opportunity to describe specific things that could contribute to the success of the technique. With this concrete picture of elements of a successful turn and talk, the collaborating teachers were better able to coach the residents on the technique, and were more likely to successfully implement the technique themselves.

In addition to the more formal support related to the practice of whole-class discussion provided through professional learning, collaborating teachers were also coached on the practice, and their support of residents' work on the practice, in more informal ways. For example, when residents attempted to facilitate a whole-class discussion, the collaborating teacher and clinical teacher educator could observe the resident together, and discuss strengths and areas of growth. Before debriefing with the resident, the collaborating teacher and clinical teacher educator shared their respective viewpoints and observations, and each learned from the other. This conversation informed the debrief with the resident, and allowed the collaborating teacher and clinical teacher educator to present the resident with aligned feedback. The clinical teacher educator might have suggested modifications the resident could try in order to more successfully lead a discussion, and suggested ways in which the collaborating teacher might continue to coach the resident on the practice. In this process, the collaborating teachers continued to broaden their thinking about the practice of whole-class discussion, and consider specific ways that it could be implemented more successfully. This work often translated to the collaborating teacher's own facilitation of whole-class discussion.

The collaborating teacher and clinical teacher educator might then continue to work together to coach the resident's work on whole-class discussion, which might involve planning meetings with the resident, in-the-moment coaching, and debriefs of observations. Throughout this process, the collaborating teacher and clinical teacher educator met to discuss the resident's progress and ways in which they might support the resident. Through this work together, the collaborating teachers continued to expand their thinking about the practice of whole-class discussion, and the clinical teacher educator learned from the collaborating teachers' on-the-ground perspective as well.

Coaching In-service Teachers in Core Practices for Document-Based History Instruction

Our second illustration of bringing core practices to the field involves a professional development program for secondary history teachers around a document-based history curriculum. In this instance, a mid-Atlantic school district was interested in reforming its secondary social studies curriculum to center on the integration and analysis of primary sources. In addition to offering formal professional development workshops to secondary teachers on the *Reading Like a Historian* curriculum (sheg.stanford. edu), one of the authors, Abby Reisman, decided to explore the design of ongoing coaching support around a specific core practice: facilitating whole-class discussions around historical texts. Her interest in this particular practice emerged from previous findings that even when teachers enthusiastically implemented document-based lessons in history, they struggled to facilitate student discourse around texts.[1]

Over the course of three years, Reisman worked with groups of teachers in different coaching arrangements, including in-person observations followed by debriefs in which teachers analyzed videotaped instruction, and virtual coaching encounters using a video-based coaching platform called *Edthena* (edthena.com).

Several takeaways emerged from the work that contribute to our understanding of how we might build coaching support for in-service teachers around core practices.

Takeaway #1: Shared language of practice. As has been articulated throughout this book, an essential starting place for any ongoing coaching focused on core practices is a common language that teachers and coaches can use to describe practice. Over the course of working with teachers in this particular context, Reisman introduced specific terms that referred to discrete moves that teachers might use in the course of facilitating discussion (e.g., textual press, revoicing), as well as broader conceptual categories that described both the content and the purpose of particular facilitation moves (e.g., orienting students to the text, orienting students to each other).[2] Both ways of describing practice proved essential in helping teachers name and identify specific strategies for fostering and supporting student discourse. The process of applying these terms and conceptual categories to videos of classroom instruction helped teachers refine their understanding of each of the moves and the range of ways to enact them.

Takeaway #2: Supporting principled curricular adaptations. Although coaching focused on the core practice of facilitating document-based discussions, there was no way to disentangle these discussions from the larger lessons in which they were embedded. For teachers whose students needed additional scaffolding to engage in discussion, these curricular adaptations often came earlier in the lesson, in the form of further modifying documents or designing reading supports that helped students develop a firmer grasp of the content and texts to be discussed. Such curricular adaptations underscore the importance of teachers understanding how the curriculum works to promote particular subject matter learning goals. Teachers had to appreciate not only that historical questions were open to interpretation, but that the documents in the *Reading Like a Historian* curriculum were specifically selected and sequenced to invite students into the process of historical inquiry. A coach who wishes to support teacher enactment of discussion must attend to the particular contexts in which teachers work in order to help teachers adapt the curriculum in principled ways that support their students' needs.

Takeaway #3: Attending to teachers' developmental trajectories. Coaches can attend to teachers' different developmental trajectories, a key benefit of including personalized coaching in any professional development program. What became immediately clear in working with groups of teachers around the core practice of facilitating discussion is that some were comfortable engaging students in discussions about history and did so with a degree of facility, and some hewed almost exclusively to traditional models of recitation and initiation-response discourse. The question for the field is how to help coaches differentiate their support to meet teachers at their level of competency with the practice. For example, two coaching methods appeared to be effective in supporting teachers who initially had little student voice in their teaching. First, those teachers appeared to benefit from concrete suggestions that they could easily and immediately incorporate into their instruction. One teacher who strictly followed an initiation-response-evaluation pattern for all of his questioning was encouraged to pause when a student responded to an open-ended question and poll the other students in the class about whether they agreed or disagreed with the first student's answer. The technique, initially a mechanical move with little follow-up, ultimately served to open the classroom discourse to flurries of student-to-student interaction. At the other end of the spectrum, teachers who have experience and comfort facilitating student discourse can be coached to further develop their practice by helping their students engage in self-sustaining and self-regulated discussions around historical documents. With such teachers, a coach's work can focus on developing the scaffolds that students might need—in the form of sentence starters or discussion prompts—that would allow the teacher to phase out their role as facilitators.

Takeaway #4: Value of classroom video. Videos of classroom instruction played an essential role in helping teachers envision and enact document-based historical discussion. Especially in the case of document-based history instruction, where history must be made open to investigation in ways that few teachers experienced in their own K–12 education, classroom videos play a critical role in illustrating what such instruction looks and sounds like. A number of projects with math teachers have explored the value of bringing teachers together in "video clubs" to analyze and discuss videos of classroom instruction.[3] In the context of coaching individual teachers, videos can be used in other ways. For example, when working with teachers over longer periods of time, juxtaposing classroom videos of their teaching can serve to prompt reflection about how their instruction has changed over time. A series of online platforms are now available to support teacher analysis of classroom videos. These platforms allow teachers and coaches to tag and comment upon specific moments in the video. The assumption underlying such analysis is that if teachers learn to identify those aspects of instruction that are most relevant to successful facilitation of discussion, they might be able to transfer this understanding to their in-the-moment decision making in the context of their own instruction. Such videos ultimately serve to broaden teachers' vista of the possible.

USING A CORE PRACTICE APPROACH IN LONG-TERM PROFESSIONAL DEVELOPMENT

The Hollyhock Fellowship is a comprehensive professional learning program for early-career teachers focused on their development of core teaching practices that lead to improved student learning for all. The program design includes a two-week institute for two consecutive summers in residence at Stanford University and monthly video-based coaching during two consecutive school years.

High school teachers from across the country teaching in schools where 50% or more of the student population qualifies for free and reduced lunch may apply to be a part of this highly competitive program. Cohorts are comprised of qualified teams that represent as much diversity as possible with regard to school context, geography, and teacher demographics. After four cohorts, 38 percent of the participants have been teachers of color.

The program focuses on supporting teachers to develop the core practices of eliciting student thinking and learning how to orchestrate productive academic discussions, in both whole-class and small-group settings, with equitable student voice and participation. Eliciting student thinking and facilitating productive discourse are complex practices that involve multiple points of in-the-moment decision making, so improving the quality of teachers' ability to elicit student thinking and facilitate productive talk requires practice of these decision-making skills. An adapted version of the Cycle for Collectively Learning[4] (see figure 7.1) is a central component of how the two-year professional learning experience is structured so that the fellows understand what these core practices look and sound like in the classroom and how these practices support student learning. In this adaptation we emphasize the role of the core practice in the classroom and use a particular pedagogy for each phase, rather than a variety of pedagogies. We also have the fellows experience phases one and two in a face-to-face setting during the summer institute. Then, during the school year, they participate in multiple passes through phases three and four with the support of an instructional coach using videoconferencing and videos of their classroom practice.

FIGURE 7.1 *Cycle for Collectively Learning as adapted for the Hollyhock Fellowship program*

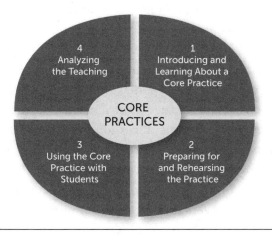

Phase One: Introducing and Learning about a Core Practice

To learn a new practice, teachers need opportunities to see clear representations of the practice through video examples or live-model lessons of
accomplished teachers. These representations help teachers distinguish
between more and less effective versions of a teaching practice.[5] During
the two summer institutes, the fellows have multiple opportunities to
both see their instructors model the core practices of eliciting student
thinking and facilitating academic discussions and to watch video ex-
emplars of these core practices. During the phase of learning a new core
practice, the fellows decompose the practice they experienced or observed
into its myriad sub-practices to develop an understanding of the individual moves that comprise the more complex practice.

Phase Two: Preparing for and Rehearsing the Activity

Taking up a new teaching practice requires opportunities to try out the
practice in a low-stakes setting. The Hollyhock summer institute is designed so that the fellows have multiple opportunities to approximate, or
rehearse, the core practice they have just experienced and decomposed.
They have time to deliberately plan for a specific core practice such as
facilitating a sense-making discussion and then rehearse the plan with a
small group of peers. The rehearsal takes place within a structured protocol in which the fellows rotate through the roles of being the rehearsing
teacher, the facilitator of the protocol, or a participating fellow.

Rehearsing fellows typically plan a fifteen-minute rehearsal using cri-
teria supplied by the instructor. They develop a planning document for
other members of the rehearsal group to preview before the discussion
begins; this document includes a context for the students and school site
and the intentional choices made for the rehearsal that are based on that
context. Rehearsals of academic discussion are typically focused at the
level of practicing "talk moves," such as ask, press, revoice, post, and connect, that encourage student-to-student interaction.

Participating fellows playing the role of students attempt to reflect the
bright spots and challenges of real students during student discussion. After the discussion these fellows provide feedback to the rehearsing fellow.

The facilitator keeps time and leads the feedback portion of the rehearsal. A facilitator may also choose to time-out or pause a particular rehearsal in order to help the rehearsing fellow move forward, rewind, or reset.

This work during the summer provides not only a rehearsal of a core practice, but an opportunity to build trust with the instructional coach and peers who will be participating in the virtual coaching that drives phases three and four. We could expect that practicing teachers would be reticent to rehearse with or in front of peers. There is certainly the possibility that rehearsing for teaching enactments could be perceived, by practicing teachers, as inauthentic or unnecessary. However, we find that teachers are willing to engage in rehearsals, perhaps because they are part and parcel of the collaborative learning model. Teachers collectively engage in a shared experience of learning discussion facilitation, observe an approximation of discussion, then prepare to enact a discussion with students. The learning cycle organizes the professional learning activity so that rehearsal is one component and, in the context of collaborative learning, is approached as an intellectual and problem-solving endeavor rather than a practice.

Phase Three: Enacting the Activity with Students

Once teachers have a deeper understanding of the complex practice of facilitating academic discussion and eliciting student thinking, they are ready to return to their classrooms to integrate that practice into their teaching. During the school year, fellows regularly record videos of their use of the core practice they learned and rehearsed during the summer. These videos are uploaded to a web platform (torshtalent.com) to use during the instructional coaching component of the program. Fellows meet via videoconference each month with their instructional coaches to discuss the ways in which they have enacted the core practices into their classroom teaching. About a third of these conference calls are individual—just a fellow with a coach, another third are designed for a "content cluster" of fellows meeting with an instructional coach, and the last third are designed for the school team. This approach extends the summer learning directly into the school year by situating the work in each teacher's classroom.

Phase Four: Analyzing Enactment and Moving Forward

The school year component of the program includes nine coaching sessions spread throughout the academic year. These sessions focus on the analysis of the enactments in the fellows' classrooms. The video-based platform supports this analysis because the video can be tagged with comments that map to specific timestamps, multiple people can make comments on the same video, the comments are color coded by individual, and supporting documents can be uploaded with the video.

As mentioned above, the analysis phase takes place in three different ways. First, a fellow works with a coach one-on-one, receiving individualized, content-specific feedback focused on specific components of facilitating productive talk and eliciting student thinking in ways that are tailored to the individual fellow's needs and development and the demands of the fellow's teaching contexts.

Second, teachers analyze some of their videos with their content cluster. The content cluster is typically a group of three teachers from different schools who teach the same subject matter and who have worked closely together during the summer institute. The teachers share videos with each other in the platform so that they can make comments on the videos that further develop their understanding of the core practice. These conversations are facilitated by an instructional coach from the same content area, with whom the fellows worked during the summer.

Third, the instructional coaches facilitate conversations with the school-based teams focused on cross-content issues of equity and how their teaching practice, particularly in orchestrating academic discussions and eliciting student thinking, is meeting the needs of students in their classes and creating opportunities for equitable student voice and participation.

Observations Based on Using a Core Practice Approach in a Multiyear Professional Learning Experience

Takeaway #1: It is possible to improve instruction by focusing on a carefully selected set of core practices. In this work, the core practice approach is tightly coupled with a philosophical approach that teachers are sophisticated instructional decision makers focused on improving the equity of learning in their classrooms. Therefore, the rehearsing, enacting, and analyzing core practices needs to be in service of that role. To accomplish this, we focus explicitly on the instructional moves teachers make and their impact on student learning in the content-specific settings.

Takeaway # 2: Situating the core practice work so that it is also strengthening pedagogical content knowledge and deepening disciplinary content knowledge is important. After one summer of attempting to teach the core practice of facilitating academic discussion across disciplines, we moved all of our core practice work into content-specific settings. We found that it was critical for teachers to understand the practices in the context of their own disciplinary framework if they were going to be able to support students' skills—in thinking, reading, writing, analyzing, and problem solving—in ways that are consistent with the study of science, mathematics, history, and literature. This approach requires teachers to delve deeper into specific areas of content in order to support student learning, and also to understand the connection between content knowledge and disciplinary practices.

Takeaway #3: A core practice approach can be leveraged to develop instructional leaders who create equitable learning opportunities for all students. We used our stance that teachers are instructional decision makers as the basis for defining being a responsive teacher. Teachers who are responsive to each student and his or her understanding of the content are more equipped to address inequities in their classrooms. Combining this view of equity with a core practice approach provides concrete, meaningful ways to understand complex instructional practices and make changes that increase student voice and improve student learning.

Takeaway #4: Using the Cycle for Collectively Learning in a sustained manner offered an authentic context for deprivatizing practice and building professional community. The nature of this program offers the luxury of building long-term relationships in which teachers build trust with colleagues around the country as well as with a small team within their school. The learning cycle offers a structure that is focused on understanding teaching practice, not critiquing teachers. By embedding the use of specific structures such as the rehearsal protocal within the cycle, teachers have a predictable, safe environment in which to take risks. By taking risks together, sharing videos, and conducting analysis of the videos, the fellows open their practice to each other and learn ways to change their practice in service of student learning.

In our ongoing studies of this program we are beginning to see evidence of uptake and teaching of specific core practices in a disciplinary context, an increase in teachers' commitment to remaining in the classroom, and student gains in interpretive discussion, confidence, and enjoyment.

USING LEARNING LABS FOR SCHOOL-BASED, JOB-EMBEDDED PROFESSIONAL DEVELOPMENT

A final brief example we want to point to is the use of the core practice approach to reorganize the professional learning opportunities of teachers within their own schools to improve both teacher and student learning outcomes. An approach that we have seen successfully combat the isolation teachers typically experience, and instead build stronger coherence and collaboration across a school, involves strong instructional leadership by principals and coaches to coordinate the following learning structures for teachers: (1) regular grade-level learning labs, (2) weekly instruction-focused grade-team meetings, (3) frequent mathematics instructional support in the classroom by both the coach and principal, and (4) weekly instructional leadership–team meetings between the coach and principal. Learning labs, organized around the now familiar learning cycle shared many times throughout this book, involve a series of half- or full-day experiences, embedded within the school day, in which small groups of teachers work with their school-based mathematics coaches to collectively plan, enact, and debrief instruction with a focus on student mathematical thinking.[6] Similar to lesson study,[7] during learning labs teachers plan and teach together. However, in a learning lab, the drafted lesson plans are less polished than in lesson study, so that teachers can regularly confer with one another during instruction as they experience how students respond to the lesson.[8] In between learning labs, teachers meet weekly in grade-level teams to reflect on student learning and teaching practice, and to make collective decisions about upcoming instruction. Crucial to the effectiveness of these structures is the attendance and active participation of the principal and the subject-area instructional coach. To coordinate their work, the principal and coach also meet in weekly meetings with other school leaders (e.g., other instructional coaches or assistant principals) to discuss teachers' development of the intended instructional practices across the school and what they can do to continue improvement and learning (see TEDD.org for resources organized around subject-specific instructional activities and how to facilitate learning labs using the structure of the learning cycle).

CONCLUSION

We hope the examples in this chapter fuel the imagination of what structures we can invent and experiment with to support teachers to learn from and with one another with clear and consistent focus on students' ideas and experiences in school. Teaching well requires a continual process of inquiry and reflection. Learning from our students and working to disrupt inequitable conditions demands time for teachers to have opportunities to learn together and from their students. Our efforts to use what we have learned as teacher educators by working on core practices has helped us to reimagine professional learning structures and improve the work lives of teachers and their abilities to serve their students well.

Coda: Learning Together

Katie A. Danielson, Sarah Schneider Kavanagh, and Elham Kazemi

In these final pages, we discuss how working together on practice has promoted opportunities for collaborative learning across teachers, teacher educators, and K–12 students. We share stories of how working together around practice has afforded us opportunities to open windows into each others' work, spark conversations about teaching with broader communities, and push *together* on some perennial challenges in teacher education. We offer this coda as an invitation to the field to engage with us in a continuation of this collaboration. Many of us have experienced this collaboration as transformational. Brad Fogo, coauthor of chapter 3, explained that for him, "Having the time and space to define teacher and teacher education practices with colleagues, to then watch them teach and enact these practices and carefully consider the planning, instructional tools, and course assignments used to support their students in learning and taking up ambitious practices has provided ideas, examples, and tools that I am developing and trying out in my own methods courses. This process has transformed my practice as a teacher educator."

We have deliberately approached this work with a view that the outcomes of our collaborations around practice have to be seen as works in progress, never finished or "right," but as responsive to efforts to address the challenges in our field and what it means to teach for a more just society. The perspectives we share below illustrate how we have used our work on practice to build bridges across the fissures that have for too long kept teacher educators apart from each other, apart from practicing teachers, and apart from K–12 students. We hope to offer to the field images of a future in which the practice of teaching can be used as an anchor for innovative collaborations—collaborations that don't *end* with the specification of practices and pedagogies, but only begin there. As chapter 3 coauthor Sarah McGrew explained, the opportunity to work with other teacher educators "expands my vision of what's possible in the courses I teach and makes working to improve my practice more fruitful, engaging, and frankly, fun."

For some, the idea that specifications of practice can lead to innovations in teacher education might seem like a contradiction in terms. How can specification lead to innovation? Isn't specifying a way of constraining, not a way of expanding? Grappling with specifications of practice, as Sarah McGrew described, has allowed us to expand the horizons of our work rather than constricting it. It has given us opportunities we hadn't expected before we began and it has given us ways of working together that weren't previously available to us. Choosing to focus on practice has forced us to listen to children and adolescents, to teachers, and to other teacher educators in new ways. Below, we offer vignettes about how our work on practice has allowed us to learn with and from K–12 students and their teachers, from our teacher candidates, and from other teacher educators.

STRAIGHT FROM THE FIELD: TEACHER EDUCATORS REFLECT ON LEARNING FROM STUDENTS AND TEACHERS

One innovation in the design of teacher preparation that many members of the CPC have explored is situating methods instruction in the field by closely partnering with classroom teachers and their students. This way of moving the learning of teaching closer to practice can be time-intensive and challenging to launch successfully, but it is grounded in creating ecologies that enable learning at many different layers, as Elizabeth Dutro and Elham Kazemi, a chapter 7 coauthor, explain about their respective courses in literacy and mathematics.

Elizabeth Dutro and Elham Kazemi

One of the central goals of our model is to design layered contexts for novices to experience particular teaching moves and anti-oppressive goals as inextricable from relationship with children and colleagues.

Our aim is for those layers to meld into a coherent ecology of impactful learning. For instance, relationships between children and novices, and the forms of advocacy they foster, are developed within collective and individual honing of core practices of teaching within a given instructional activity. In turn, knowledge of and care for a child impacts the kinds of teaching moves and support for participation that novices enact in their instruction. The close work with children provides novices with an opportunity to experience in one quarter or semester a taste of the knowledge and rapport that must be built with children in order to enact teaching moves that value children's knowledge and interrupt deficit assumptions that some may bring. Making these layers of learning available requires intention in design and mediation in enactment. Further, we are struck by how sustaining a partnership with a school not only provides us with opportunities to build relationships with children, teachers, and school staff across years, but allows new cohorts of preservice teachers to enter a school feeling they are part of a known and valued history.

Andrea Bien, another chapter 7 coauthor, shares further reflections on the opportunities for teacher educator learning afforded by such work.

Andrea Bien

One of the central tenets of my work with teachers is that making practice public has value. Working on teaching with teachers (both in- and preservice) and students (both university and elementary) in the field has generated countless opportunities to teach publicly and to learn through those enactments of teaching. One of these learning experiences stands out as particularly powerful because it led to shifts in my thinking about how to make more of my own practice not only public, but transparent to my preservice teachers.

One semester I taught an Elementary Literacy methods course in a school in collaboration with an especially wonderful second grade teacher, Sarah Dietz. She was a graduate of our program and had an understanding of the place-based methods course model that, I think, positioned her to offer particularly keen insights. It seems likely I was also at a place in my own trajectory of learning as a teacher educator that I was able to shift my practice with the knowledge I gained through her insights.

One of the instructional activities I used in the methods class was Word Work. The week I was modeling a word sort for my preservice teachers, Sarah's second grade class was working on contractions. So, I modeled a whole-class word sort on contractions from one of the *Words Their Way* books. I remember vividly that one of the greatest successes of that lesson was that one of Sarah's students, who read well below grade level and received special education services for reading and writing, shined during the lesson. The focus on contractions enabled the student to think abstractly and demonstrate understanding in ways she was not typically able to do in small-group word sorts that targeted phonological patterns for beginning readers. It was Sarah who noticed this. Sarah shared her insider knowledge of her student after we noted her engagement during the lesson. She highlighted the ways that this lesson gave her students new and different points of access to word study than some of the small-group lessons afforded.

What is notable is that during the post-lesson reflection, Sarah shared that she was initially skeptical about doing a whole-class word sort. She was accustomed to doing word sorts in small groups, but she was willing to take the risk in this scenario. We informally, but thoughtfully, reflected together on the logic underlying each of our initial perspectives on lesson focus and design, and we identified the shifts that occurred during and after the enactment that, ultimately, expanded our thinking. We had not made our thinking as visible to each other before the lesson as we did in that debrief. We talked together about the shift that occurred in Sarah's thinking after seeing her student from a new perspective during the whole-class word sort, and about the ways that Sarah's knowledge of her students supported me to more deeply understand the student's participation and learning.

As Sarah and I talked together about what we learned, it struck me that that I was consistently making my teaching enactments public, but not always doing so with my planning and problem solving. Sarah and I collaboratively discussed decision making about when and how to plan whole-class or small-group word sort lessons and the affordances and constraints of these different models of instruction. That conversation made our thinking about teaching and learning more transparent to each other than my model lesson had on its own. I knew it was important to make this transparent exchange of ideas available to our preservice teachers—beyond simply decomposing the model—to give them the same window into the complexity of teaching.

My collegial relationship with Sarah and the opportunity to teach her students in her classroom generated an opportunity for me to collaboratively puzzle through teaching decisions, but that puzzling came later and was obscured to our teacher education students. I now make my decision making about approximations of practice as visible as I can to our teacher education students. My conceptualization of "making practice public" has expanded to include the complex decision making that is an integral part of teaching.

STRAIGHT FROM THE FIELD: TEACHER EDUCATORS REFLECT ON LEARNING FROM TEACHER CANDIDATES

As teacher educators, centering our pedagogy on practice has meant offering teacher candidates more frequent and better scaffolded opportunities to approximate and enact teaching practices. We've transformed our pedagogy in these ways because we believed it would be supportive of novice teacher learning. What we did not anticipate is that we, as teacher educators, would have the opportunity to learn things about practice and about learning to teach that had previously been obscured to us. Below, we offer reflections from two teacher educators describing what they have learned from watching their teacher candidates try on practice.

Sarah Schneider Kavanagh

The first teacher education courses that I taught were multicultural education courses. Our discussions in these courses were rich, and the teacher candidates I supported were engaged and thoughtful, but something was missing. Through participating in the CPC, I saw my colleagues facilitating rehearsals, supporting candidates to analyze video, and bringing candidates into classrooms to try things out with

K–12 students. I saw how my colleagues were able to gather information about what their candidates were actually able to do with young people, and I realized what was lacking in my own practice. I realized that I needed to design ways to support my candidates in transforming their sophisticated ideas into practical action with their students. The work I do with candidates is very different today. The heady discussions I used to have with my teacher candidates about the whiteness, maleness, and straightness of the curricular canon have not disappeared, but now they are paired with visits to kindergarten classrooms to read aloud books with queer characters of color. We still have conversations about how prejudices get reproduced in school environments, but now those conversations are paired with rehearsals of responding to students' prejudiced remarks. The biggest surprise of this transformation has been how much I've been able to learn about the complexity of teaching for social justice by watching my teacher candidates try to put their ideas into action. Practice-based pedagogy has offered me a window into what my candidates are actually able to do with children. Through this window, I see things about their practice (and my own) that I never could have seen before. For example, when watching a candidate struggle through a text-based discussion of a book about a family with two dads, I realized that none of the conversations we had had in the teacher education classroom had set my candidate up to engage with children's thinking about gender, families, and love. We had spent so much time unpacking how sociologists think that I had forgotten to engage my teacher candidates with how five-year-olds think. I've found that every time I've opened myself up to an opportunity to see my teacher candidates teach, I've learned something that has helped me improve my practice as a teacher educator.

Chauncey Monte-Sano

As I've been involved in the CPC, I've specified core practices I aim to teach candidates with more precision, and I have used those specifications to analyze my candidates' videos of practice and discuss their videos with others. Through that process, I've been able to see more clearly what my candidates take up and what they do not take up. For example, I've noticed that when modeling, candidates learned specific steps to take and executed them, but they often lost a sense of purpose for modeling and didn't always connect modeling to the larger goals of the lesson, making it hard to understand what the strategy being modeled was for. This realization led me to revise how I was defining modeling, provide a structure for their assignment that guided candidates to integrate modeling more meaningfully into lessons, and revise some of the activities we did together to work in this core practice. Talking with others who have viewed the same videos has pushed me to systematically notice candidates' strengths and areas for improvement, identify patterns in candidates' uptake, and revise my specification and supporting curriculum to better support candidates.

STRAIGHT FROM THE FIELD: TEACHER EDUCATORS REFLECT ON LEARNING FROM OTHER TEACHER EDUCATORS

By specifying practice we offered ourselves a common language around which we could collaborate. Without naming and specifying the practical things we were going to try together, we would have struggled to try on comparable pedagogical approaches. What we did not realize in advance was that specifying practice gave us a way to look through the window at a common landscape. Below, we offer reflections from two consortium members sharing their learnings from other teacher educators in the group.

Lightning Jay

I remember watching a video of Abby Reisman modeling discussion facilitation with a group of teacher candidates. I listened to how she spoke to candidates, what she chose to make explicit, and how she pivoted between her roles as discussion leader, professor, and supportive coach for these novice teachers. Videos like that gave me vivid examples of expert instruction to emulate. Other videos showed me a variety of representations, instructional activities, and instructional styles that continue to influence my practice. Rather than being limited to my own experience, video has allowed me to draw from more institutions and teacher educators than I could ever hope to visit in person. As someone who never attended a program similar to the one where I currently teach, I was concerned about being an outsider. Mentors have helped me overcome that concern, and video has increased my access to mentors.

Mark Windschitl

It was a privilege to be allowed into the classrooms of two fellow teacher educators to observe them working with their novice educators on sense-making discussions. As I watched video of Matt [Kloser]'s rehearsals at Notre Dame, I could feel the familiar tensions when each of his candidates walked to the front of the room in the role of the teacher, took a deep breath, and tried out a kind of responsive pedagogy that is not common in schools today. As each rehearsal unfolded, I took note of when Matt paused the action and how he gently provided support in those moments or challenged his novices to try a replay. Matt's own practice as a teacher educator was something I could check against my own: Why did he stop the rehearsals in certain places? Do I use the same repertoire of moves after I pause my novices? Did his novices, who took their turns at teaching later, benefit from observing peers who went before them? Andrea Wells's classroom in the teacher residency setting had its own unique energy. Her novices brought a sense of urgency to the rehearsals because, for them, their simulated lessons would be retaught the next day, somewhere in a Boston public school with thirty or so real students. I observed how Andrea allowed longer, more free-form discussions when she paused her young teachers in mid-dialogue. She let her whole class problematize the moment of practice they were experiencing, and they often talked about how the moves would work with students they each knew, occasionally gesturing to an empty chair as though the student were sitting in the room with them—"So, how will your pressing and probing work with Jamel?" From watching my peers, I came to understand that practices like sense-making discussions can be things that we name and specify on paper. They can even be the objects of dispassionate analysis. But enacting them with learners, whether these are one's peers in a teacher education program or middle school students in a classroom, is a nuanced and complex undertaking. Technical skills are not enough; they must be combined with humility, a willingness to learn from failure, and a desire to humanize the learning space entrusted to you. I am speaking here not only about our young teachers, but also about us as teacher educators.

OPENING UP POSSIBILITIES

The ideas in this book are works in progress. The voices of teacher educators that we shared in this coda convey the value of collaborating across subject areas, across grade levels, across roles, and across institutions. Meghan Shaughnessy, a chapter 4 co-author, and Betsy Davis, a chapter 5 co-author, underscored the unifying experience of engaging in deliberations about programmatic redesign by trying to identify common pillars and high-leverage practices for their teacher education program. When we asked our colleagues to share what they learned by having an opportunity to work together, we heard repeatedly about how much everyone felt they had grown. As Matt Kloser explained, what might have started for some as an opportunity to conduct research quickly expanded to tackle the problem of isolation that teacher educators in higher education experience. "While experiences in academia vary from institution to institution, the practice of opening up one's teaching to external feedback and critique is less than common. As teacher educators, we recognize the importance of a classroom teachers' personal reflection on, mentoring with, and observations of one's instructional practice. Yet too often, these essential elements of professional growth are eschewed in postsecondary contexts." The CPC leveraged opportunities for both research and professional growth, and as chapter 6 coauthor Ashley Cartun put it, the opportunity became "a game changer."

We hope this book encourages teacher educators to continue to seek ways of building and expanding networks to learn from each other, from teacher candidates, and from students. By engaging in these collaborations, we can continue to improve the experiences of novices in our teacher education programs and shape the work environments that we need in our institutions to continue to serve our students well.

APPENDIX

TeachingWorks' High-Leverage Practices[1]

Tie to rubric

- **Leading a group discussion** *and go more-making*

  In a group discussion, the teacher and all of the students work on specific content together, using one another's ideas as resources. The purposes of a discussion are to build collective knowledge and capability in relation to specific instructional goals and to allow students to practice listening, speaking, and interpreting. The teacher and a wide range of students contribute orally, listen actively, and respond to and learn from others' contributions.

- **Explaining and modeling content, practices, and strategies**

  Explaining and modeling are practices for making a wide variety of content, academic practices, and strategies explicit to students. Depending on the topic and the instructional purpose, teachers might rely on simple verbal explanations, sometimes with accompanying examples or representations. In teaching more complex academic practices and strategies, such as an algorithm for carrying out a mathematical operation or the use of metacognition to improve reading comprehension, teachers might choose a more elaborate kind of explanation that we are calling "modeling." Modeling includes verbal explanation, but also thinking aloud and demonstrating.

- **Eliciting and interpreting individual students' thinking** */ musing*

  Teachers pose questions or tasks that provoke or allow students to share their thinking about specific academic content in order to evaluate student understanding, guide instructional decisions, and surface ideas that will benefit other students. To do this effectively, a teacher draws out a student's thinking through carefully chosen questions and tasks and considers and checks alternative interpretations of the student's ideas and methods.

- **Diagnosing particular common patterns of student thinking and development in a subject-matter domain**

  (handwritten annotation: anticipating challenge)

  Although there are important individual and cultural differences among students, there are also common patterns in the ways in which students think about and develop understanding and skill in relation to particular topics and problems. Teachers who are familiar with common patterns of student thinking and development, and who are fluent in anticipating or identifying them, are able to work more effectively and efficiently as they plan and implement instruction and evaluate student learning.

- **Implementing norms and routines for classroom discourse and work**

  Each discipline has norms and routines that reflect the ways in which people in the field construct and share knowledge. These norms and routines vary across subjects but often include establishing hypotheses, providing evidence for claims, and showing one's thinking in detail. Teaching students what they are, why they are important, and how to use them is crucial to building understanding and capability in a given subject. Teachers may use explicit explanation, modeling, and repeated practice to do this.

- **Coordinating and adjusting instruction during a lesson**

  Teachers must take care to coordinate and adjust instruction during a lesson in order to maintain coherence, ensure that the lesson is responsive to students' needs, and use time efficiently. This includes explicitly connecting parts of the lesson, managing transitions carefully, and making changes to the plan in response to student progress.

- **Specifying and reinforcing productive student behavior**

  Clear expectations for student behavior and careful work on the teacher's part to teach productive behavior to students, reward it, and strategically redirect off-task behavior help create classrooms that are productive learning environments for all. This practice includes not only skills for laying out classroom rules and managing truly disruptive behavior, but for recognizing the many ways that children might act when they actually are engaged and for teaching students how to interact with each other and the teacher while in class.

- **Implementing organizational routines**
  Teachers implement routine ways of carrying out classroom tasks in order to maximize the time available for learning and minimize disruptions and distractions. They organize time, space, materials, and students strategically, and deliberately teach students how to complete tasks such as lining up at the door, passing out papers, and asking to participate in class discussion. This can include demonstrating and rehearsing routines and maintaining them consistently.

- **Setting up and managing small group work**
  Teachers use small group work when instructional goals call for in-depth interaction among students and in order to teach students to work collaboratively. To use groups effectively, teachers choose tasks that require and foster collaborative work, issue clear directions that permit groups to work semi-independently, and implement mechanisms for holding students accountable for both collective and individual learning. They use their own time strategically, deliberately choosing which groups to work with, when, and on what.

- **Building respectful relationships with students**
  Teachers increase the likelihood that students will engage and persist in school when they establish positive, individual relationships with them. Techniques for doing this include greeting students positively every day, having frequent, brief, "check in" conversations with students to demonstrate care and interest, and following up with students who are experiencing difficult or special personal situations.

- **Talking about a student with parents or other caregivers**
  Regular communication between teachers and parents/guardians supports student learning. Teachers communicate with parents to provide information about students' academic progress, behavior, or development; to seek information and help; and to request parental involvement in school. These communications may take place in

person, in writing, or over the phone. Productive communications are attentive to considerations of language and culture and designed to support parents and guardians in fostering their child's success in and out of school.

- **Learning about students' cultural, religious, family, intellectual, and personal experiences and resources for use in instruction**
  Teachers must actively learn about their particular students in order to design instruction that will meet their needs. This includes being deliberate about trying to understand the cultural norms for communicating and collaborating that prevail in particular communities, how certain cultural and religious views affect what is considered appropriate in school, and the topics and issues that interest individual students and groups of students. It also means keeping track of what is happening in students' personal lives so as to be able to respond appropriately when an out-of-school experience affects what is happening in school.

- **Setting long- and short-term learning goals for students**
  Clear goals referenced to external standards help teachers ensure that all students learn expected content. Explicit goals help teachers to maintain coherent, purposeful, and equitable instruction over time. Setting effective goals involves analysis of student knowledge and skills in relation to established standards and careful efforts to establish and sequence interim benchmarks that will help ensure steady progress toward larger goals.

- **Designing single lessons and sequences of lessons**
  Carefully sequenced lessons help students develop deep understanding of content and sophisticated skills and practices. Teachers design and sequence lessons with an eye toward providing opportunities for student inquiry and discovery, and include opportunities for students to practice and master foundational concepts and skills before moving on to more advanced ones. Effectively sequenced lessons maintain a coherent focus while keeping students engaged; they also help students achieve appreciation of what they have learned.

- **Checking student understanding during and at the conclusion of lessons**
  Teachers use a variety of informal but deliberate methods to assess what students are learning during and between lessons. These frequent checks provide information about students' current level of competence and help the teacher adjust instruction during a single lesson or from one lesson to the next. They may include, for example, simple questioning, short performance tasks, or journal or notebook entries.

- **Selecting and designing formal assessments of student learning**
  Effective summative assessments provide teachers with rich information about what students have learned and where they are struggling in relation to specific learning goals. In composing and selecting assessments, teachers consider validity, fairness, and efficiency. Effective summative assessments provide both students and teachers with useful information and help teachers evaluate and design further instruction.

- **Interpreting the results of student work, including routine assignments, quizzes, tests, projects, and standardized assessments**
  Student work is the most important source of information about the effectiveness of instruction. Teachers must analyze student productions, including assessments of all kinds, looking for patterns that will guide their efforts to assist specific students and the class as a whole and inform future instruction.

- **Providing oral and written feedback to students**
  Effective feedback helps focus students' attention on specific qualities of their work; it highlights areas needing improvement, and delineates ways to improve. Good feedback is specific, not overwhelming in scope, focused on the academic task, and supports students' perceptions of their own capability. Giving skillful feedback requires the teacher to make strategic choices about the frequency, method, and content of feedback and to communicate in ways that are understandable by students.

- **Analyzing instruction for the purpose of improving it**

  Learning to teach is an ongoing process that requires regular analysis of instruction and its effectiveness. Teachers study their own teaching and that of their colleagues in order to improve their understanding of the complex interactions between teachers, students, and content and of the impact of particular instructional approaches. Analyzing instruction may take place individually or collectively and involves identifying salient features of the instruction and making reasoned hypotheses for how to improve.

The Core Practices
of the University of
Washington's U-ACT Program[2]

- **Positioning students as competent sense-makers**
  Getting students to risk putting their ideas on the table requires you
  to express curiosity about all of their ideas, not just the "right" ones.
  Teachers express curiosity about students' ideas both through how
  they ask questions to elicit student thinking and how they respond to
  students' ideas. In order to position students as competent participants
  in a discussion, you have to ask questions that students can answer.
  In addition, if students are expected to have accurate and sophisticated ideas every time they share, they will learn quickly to keep their
  mouths shut until they are 100 percent sure about what it is you want
  to hear. The way that you react to students' unfinished, emergent,
  or inaccurate ideas is like a neon sign to your students indicating
  whether your classroom is a safe place to take intellectual risks. In
  addition, notice that it's impossible to position students as competent
  sense-makers if you aren't positioning them as sense-makers, which
  requires that we design tasks and ask questions that engage students in
  reasoning and disciplinary practices.

- **Teaching towards an instructional goal**
  Your instructional goal is like the North Star. As you and your students launch into discussion, you will wander through a variety of
  ideas—some you can anticipate in advance and some you cannot. As
  the teacher, your job throughout that wandering is to always have
  your eye on the North Star of your instructional goal. Your goal will
  help you decide what you're listening for in your students' talk, which
  ideas you want everyone to delve into together, and which ideas
  you're okay with leaving for another day.

- **Eliciting and responding to student thinking**

  Meaningful learning cannot occur if you don't first elicit students' thinking. Without eliciting student thinking, you cannot learn about your students' prior experiences, current understandings, interests, needs, and language. Often when teachers begin to work on this core practice, they find that when they think they are eliciting students' thinking, they are really just asking students to recall facts or to find a correct answer that is sitting somewhere right in front of them. Productive talk can only begin if you ask students to share what *they're* thinking—not what *you're* thinking. This requires posing open-ended questions that ask students to make sense of a shared problem, artifact, text, or phenomenon. It also requires responding to the ideas that students share in ways that propel classroom talk instead of shutting it down. Responding productively to student thinking requires careful listening and the ability to recognize the meaning in students' contributions and how those contributions might productively be used.

- **Orienting students to each other's ideas**

  Why do you want students to talk to one another instead of to you? For a million reasons! First, just like every teacher, you have a handful of students whose hands are always in the air and if you're not careful, these kids become the only ones whose ideas get heard. When you start getting students to turn and talk to one another, it's much easier to get everyone engaged in generating and sharing ideas. Second, the more you push students to use one another's ideas as resources, the easier it is to generate discussion where one idea builds on the next, instead of talk that feels like a series of presentations and disconnected ideas. Third, many students in your room are nervous to share their ideas. When you assign competence to students' ideas by raising up their contributions and naming them as useful to the class, you encourage students to take intellectual risks.

- **Orienting students to the content**

  It's possible to make students feel like competent sense-makers, to get them engaged in productive talk, and even to steer them towards an instructional goal without orienting them towards the BIG IDEAS of the discipline or towards disciplinary practices—that is, disciplinary ways of working, constructing knowledge, and communicating. The most basic way that you can orient students to the content is to press your students to engage in disciplinary practices (e.g., supporting their claims with evidence). At a more nuanced level, when you orient students to the content, you turn comments like this: "that's an interesting insight, Destiny" into comments like this: "I want to point out what Destiny just did because it's central to the work of a historian: she looked for similar evidence across two primary source documents, and she matched that evidence up. We call that corroboration." When we orient students to the content, we shine a light on what is most important in what they're discussing, name those things for them, and connect them to a larger purpose. Notice that it is impossible to do that work if we don't ask a question or pose a task that engages students in disciplinary practice in the first place.

- **Assessing student understanding**
  Productive discussions are powerful sites for learning about your students. One reason you want students sharing their ideas is that you can learn about how they're thinking about the content under study, which in turn will inform your instructional next steps. Meaningful instruction always builds on students' current understanding. Without knowing what and how our students are thinking, we cannot ask productive questions or press them in meaningful ways. Teachers assess their students outside of whole-class discussions using written work or through strategies such as conferencing, but assessment also happens during and through classroom talk as teachers ask productive questions to elicit students' ideas, ask follow-up questions to make sure they understand how the student is thinking, and respond in ways that provide the student with feedback either from the teacher or from other students as their thinking is opened up to other people for discussion. Teachers conduct assessments to determine how individual students are making sense of the content, as well as to determine patterns of thinking in the class that can inform instructional next steps.

For example, here are some questions you might ask yourself during a discussion that might drive your assessment in the moment: Do my students have sufficient understanding of this task or concept in order to be released to independent work? Have my students demonstrated sufficient understanding that I feel comfortable moving on to the next stage of the activity? Do my students require additional challenge? Do my students have the language they will need in order to communicate their thinking about this concept to each other during the next stage of the lesson? Is there a big misconception in the room that we need to address?

- **Creating and maintaining a productive learning environment**
  The work of creating and maintaining a productive learning environment is the bedrock under everything you do as a teacher. It includes the countless invisible things you do every day to make it possible for students to participate in meaningful activity. When you hold the read-aloud book so that everyone can see the pictures, or when you pass out copies of the short story so that students can point to textual evidence in discussion, you're making sure that students have the resources they need to participate. When you say "with a raised hand, who can build on what Marcus just said," or "when I say the magic word, turn and talk to your partner—knees to knees, eyes to eyes— about patterns that you notice in the numbers," you're ensuring that everyone knows how to share their ideas. When you move the desks so that everyone can see each other (and while you're at it, put Ben on the other side of the room from Dustin), you're organizing your classroom and your students in ways that facilitate the kind of participation that you're seeking. The core practice of creating and maintaining a productive learning environment also includes all of the ways that you make sure your students know that you and their classmates will treat their ideas with respect, and all of the ways you hold students accountable to expectations.

Protocol for Language Arts Teaching Observation 5.0: Core Practices for English Language Arts Instruction[3]

The practice of *Clarifying **Purpose*** attempts to capture both the coherence of the lesson around a communicated objective (internal learning goal) and the position of the lesson within a larger context (situated learning goal). The internal learning goal speaks to lesson structure and the relevance of classroom activities toward meeting a learning goal identified by the teacher. Situated purpose speaks to the future relevance to motivate the students to engage with the task at hand. The element focuses on whether the purpose of the lesson is made explicit by the teacher, is tied to the goals of English language arts (ELA) instruction, and is reflected in the activities undertaken by the class.

The practice of *Setting and Maintaining **Intellectual Challenge*** focuses on how teachers set the intellectual rigor of the activities and assignments in which students engage. Activities and assignments with high intellectual challenge ask students to engage in analytic or inferential thinking. Activities and content with low challenge, in contrast, require students to engage in recall or rote thinking. Intellectual challenge also depends on the level of analytical or inferential thinking demanded in the questions asked by the teacher within discussion or in class activities.

The practice of ***Representing Content*** focuses on the teacher's ability and accuracy in representing ELA content (reading, writing, literature, grammar/mechanics, and oral communications) to students through effective and meaningful explanations, examples, and analogies, along with the conceptual richness of the teacher's instructional explanations.

The practice of *Making* Connections to Prior Academic Knowledge focuses on the extent to which new material is connected to students' previous academic knowledge. When enacted well, new material explicitly builds on prior academic knowledge to develop skills, strategies, and conceptual understandings within a knowledge domain in order to meet the lesson's goals.

The practice of *Drawing* Connections to Personal and Cultural Experiences focuses on the extent to which teachers connect new material to students' personal and cultural experiences. When done well, teachers make linkages that engage students in a lesson, pique their interest in a topic, and illustrate ideas and concepts within English language arts.

The practice of Modeling and Use of Models focuses on the ways in which a teacher visibly enacts strategies, skills, and processes targeted in the lesson to guide students' work before or while they complete the task; the extent to which they are analyzed or not; and whether they are used to illustrate for students what constitutes good work on a given task. The teacher might model metacognitive or discussion strategies, a think-aloud on how to identify theme, demonstrating how to support a statement with textual evidence, and so on. Modeling often includes think-aloud and role-plays. This practice also includes the use of models to support students in completing the task at hand, such as the use of mentor texts in the teaching of writing.

The practice of *Providing* Strategy Instruction focuses on the teacher's ability to teach strategies and skills that support students in reading, writing, speaking, listening, and engaging with literature. ELA strategies may help students complete such tasks as reading for meaning, generating ideas for writing, or figuring out the meaning of unfamiliar words.

The practice of *Providing* Feedback focuses on the quality of feedback teachers provide in response to student application of ELA skills, concepts, or strategies. Feedback includes teacher comments on the quality or nature of student work as well as suggestions for how students can improve the quality of their work. High quality feedback is specific and targets the skills at the heart of the activity. The feedback helps students understand the quality of their work and helps students better perform the task at hand by addressing substantive elements of the task.

The practice of *Facilitating* Classroom Discourse focuses on the opportunities teachers create for students to have extended ELA-related talk with the teacher or among peers, and the extent to which the teacher and other students pick up on, build on, and clarify each other's ideas. At the highest level, students engage in elaborated, coherent, and focused discussions, in which the teacher and other students build on each other's contributions and prompt each other to clarify and specify their ideas.

The practice of *Engaging in* Text-Based Instruction assesses the degree to which teachers provide opportunities for students to engage in activities and discourse that are grounded in authentic texts. The practice captures the degree to which students use authentic texts and engage in the production of them. At the highest level, the teacher is using the text in the service of a larger goal: the development of readers and writers. Students actively use authentic texts for a sustained period of time to deepen their understanding of the text and wider genre and/or engage in writing authentic texts for a sustained period of time with attention to specific features of style and genre.

The practice of *Providing* Accommodations for Language Learning focuses on the range of strategies and supports that a teacher might use to make a lesson accessible to non-native English speakers or native speakers struggling to develop ELA skills. These accommodations take into account individual students' levels of language proficiency and can include a strategic use of primary language, differentiated materials (pictures, other visuals, or hands-on materials), as well as graphic organizers and visual displays to make texts and instruction accessible to all students. When done well, teachers effectively modify assignments and assessments so that all students successfully meet the ELA goals for the lesson, despite their level of language proficiency.

The practice of *Managing* Behavior focuses on the degree to which behavior management facilitates academic work and is concerned with behavioral norms and consequences. This component does not presume that an ideal classroom is a quiet and controlled one. The key question is whether student behavior is appropriate for the task at hand; an "orderly" classroom will look different during a lecture than it would during small-group work.

The practice of *Managing* Time for Instruction focuses on the amount of time students are engaged in ELA focused activity. It looks at the teacher's efficient organization of classroom routines and materials to ensure that little class time is lost and that instructional time is maximized.

Core Practices
of Science Teaching[4]

- **Engaging students in investigations**
  The teacher engages students in investigations of the material world—both investigations planned by the teacher and those planned by students. Fluency with this practice is demonstrated by the teacher providing opportunities for students to investigate phenomena and engage in the practices of science that include the posing of questions, collecting and analyzing data, arguing from evidence, building explanations, and communicating ideas about the claims and evidence tied to the investigation. Furthermore, this practice focuses on how well the investigation facilitates understanding of a core scientific or engineering idea, crosscutting concept, or practice.

- **Facilitating classroom discourse**
  The teacher creates opportunities for students to engage in science-related talk with the teacher and among peers. Fluency with this practice is demonstrated by the teacher providing opportunities for small-group and whole-class discussion; facilitating students' sharing of evidence- and/or model-based explanations and arguments; and encouraging students to take up, clarify, and justify the ideas of others. Furthermore, this practice focuses on the extent to which the teacher can establish the normative rules for discourse between students and model common discursive practices used in science.

- **Eliciting, assessing, and using student thinking about science**
  The teacher elicits student thinking about scientific concepts and practices. Fluency with this practice is demonstrated by the teacher effectively probing student thinking, both formally and informally, and through a variety of assessment practices—such as questioning—identifying students' mental models and conceptions of the material

world and scientific practices, and using this information to guide future instruction.

- **Providing feedback to students**
  The teacher provides specific verbal and/or written feedback as well as opportunities for peer or self-reflection on students' understanding and/or use of science and engineering core ideas, crosscutting concepts, and practices. Fluency with this practice is demonstrated by the teacher providing feedback and opportunities for peer and self-evaluation based on student thinking. Such feedback should provide formative advice about the quality of the student's work and progress toward the learning goal.

- **Constructing and interpreting models**
  The teacher provides opportunities for students to interpret, construct, test, revise, and use scientific models that help develop explanations for natural phenomena. Fluency with this practice is demonstrated by the teacher's use of various models (e.g., physical, analogical, abstract) as part of understanding science and engineering ideas and practices. Furthermore, fluency is demonstrated by how the teacher helps students devise, revise, and use models for the development of evidence-based explanations.

- **Connecting science to its applications**
  The teacher connects core ideas, crosscutting concepts, and practices with applications relevant to students' everyday experiences. Fluency with this practice is demonstrated by the teacher engaging students in discussions or activities that integrate the significance of scientific accounts and practices in students' daily lives and the world around them, including connections to science in current events, the historical context of science, and STS (science, technology, and society) issues.

- **Linking science concepts to phenomena**
  The teacher engages students with real-world phenomena and organisms through demonstrations, hands-on activities, and laboratory investigations, and provides multiple opportunities for students to develop a scientific understanding of the phenomena. Fluency with this

practice is demonstrated by the teacher choosing phenomena related to scientific and engineering concepts and connecting to students' prior knowledge, so as to create opportunities for students to use models and theories as explanatory tools and develop a deeper understanding of the material world.

- **Focusing on core science ideas, crosscutting concepts and practices**
  The teacher plans lessons and units that integrate the core science or engineering ideas (e.g., biological evolution), concepts that cut within and across disciplines (e.g., energy flows), and scientific and engineering practices (e.g., engaging in argument from evidence). Fluency with this practice is demonstrated by the teacher providing instruction, activities, and assessments that connect and focus on ideas of and about science and engineering that are central to developing deep understanding across disciplines.

- **Building classroom community**
  The teacher creates and maintains a safe, collaborative, learning community wherein students are willing to venture ideas, discuss their confusions, participate regardless of language level or perceived limitation, adhere to class norms, and work together toward common learning goals. Fluency with this practice is demonstrated by the teacher establishing and maintaining expectations for respectful behavior in the classroom and lab as well as providing support for discursive participation in science learning activities from all students.

- **Adapting instruction**
  The teacher uses data that indicate students' scientific knowledge and ability to engage in scientific practices to adapt and revise future instruction. Fluency with this practice is demonstrated by the teacher recognizing the learning needs of students and adapting instructional methods or the instructional plan to match those needs. Decisions are based on students' partial and alternate understandings of scientific concepts as well as the academic language needs of students.

Teaching Practices for Historical Inquiry[5]

- **Use historical questions**

  The teacher plans lessons and units around historical questions. This practice focuses on the use of questions that have driven historical scholarship and debate (e.g., Was Reconstruction about emancipation or reconciliation? Could the United States have avoided involvement in World War I? How did the Chinese Communists succeed in establishing the People's Republic of China?) to organize instruction. Further, this practice involves presenting questions focused on historical analysis that elicit and support the development of students' historical thinking and understanding, raising questions in response to students' ideas, and creating opportunities for students to generate their own historical questions.

- **Select and adapt historical sources**

  The teacher centers instruction on appropriate and engaging historical sources that include various types of texts and artifacts and illustrate multiple perspectives and interpretations. Sources should include both primary and secondary texts and may include images, political cartoons, documentaries, movies, graphs/charts, and maps. This practice also focuses on how the teacher prepares and/or adapts historical sources—such as excerpting documents or utilizing scaffolding questions—to help make them accessible to students.

- **Explain and connect historical content**

  The teacher uses historically appropriate and comprehensible explanations to describe and connect historical content, concepts, and accounts. This practice includes how the teacher uses various tools (e.g., timelines, maps, films) and strategies (e.g., lectures, storytelling, examples, analogies) to help students develop knowledge of different periods of history and specific historical contexts. When appropriate, the teacher connects historical content and concepts to the personal and cultural experiences of students and also helps students see the distinctions between their personal and cultural experiences and the historical content under study. This practice includes making relevant connections between historical and contemporary events and phenomena.

- **Model and support historical reading skills**
  The teacher models and provides students opportunities for guided and independent practice of discipline-specific reading skills. This practice focuses on how the teacher illustrates and supports different historical reading skills, such as evaluating and comparing different source materials, considering the historical context in which different artifacts and documents were created, or corroborating evidence and historical accounts.

- **Employ historical evidence**
  The teacher demonstrates the use of evidence in addressing historical questions and developing and evaluating historical claims. This practice focuses on how the teacher uses, and supports students in using, multiple forms of evidence—for example, both primary and secondary sources, visuals, maps, charts, and graphs—to develop and support historical claims and understand the connections between claims and evidence.

- **Use historical concepts**
  The teacher plans lessons and units that focus instruction on first- and second-order historical concepts (e.g., nationalism, revolution, cause and effect, change and continuity, chronology, significance). The teacher illustrates how historical content explored in class connects to, or is representative of, historical concepts and creates opportunities for students to engage in conceptual analysis of historical events, sources, and artifacts.

- **Facilitate discussion on historical topics**
  The teacher creates opportunities for students to engage in extended discussion with teachers and among peers about historical questions,

controversies, sources, or artifacts. This practice focuses on how the teacher demonstrates—and has students practice—considering, clarifying, presenting, and supporting ideas and comments with evidence, and the extent to which discussion is grounded in historical questions, texts, or artifacts.

- **Model and support historical writing**
  The teacher models and creates opportunities for students to develop and communicate historical analysis through writing. This practice focuses on the extent to which the teacher designs classroom activities that support students in using writing conventions to construct historical accounts, formulate historical claims and arguments, address counterarguments, and use evidence.

- **Assess student thinking about history**
  The teacher crafts and implements formative and summative assessments that gather valid information about students' ability to engage in historical analysis and understanding of historical accounts and concepts. This practice focuses on the extent to which a teacher identifies and evaluates student thinking and provides feedback to help students improve their historical knowledge, reasoning, and communication.

CPC's Initial Definition of Core Practices

Identifiable components of teaching that teachers enact to support learning. These components include instructional strategies and the subcomponents of routines and moves. Core practices can include both general and content-specific practices.

CPC's Initial Definition of Facilitating Discussion as a Core Practice

In a whole-class discussion, the teacher and all of the students work on specific content together, using one another's ideas as resources. The purposes of a discussion are to build collective knowledge and capability in relation to specific instructional goals and to allow students to practice listening, speaking, and interpreting. In instructionally productive discussions, the teacher and a wide range of students contribute orally, listen actively, and respond to and learn from others' contributions.

English Language Arts Specification of Facilitating Discussion

- **Definition/description of facilitating ELA discussion**

  Facilitating discussion is characterized by opportunities for students to have extended interactions with the teacher and their peers around the content. Key features of these interactions are the extent to which class members engage with the ideas presented by others (e.g., uptake, extension, probing, clarification). The goal of these opportunities is to build collective knowledge and capability in relation to specific instructional goals and to allow students to practice listening, speaking, and interpreting. In instructionally productive discourse, the teacher and a wide range of students contribute orally, listen actively, and respond to and learn from others' contributions.

ASPECTS OF FACILITATING ELA DISCUSSION

ASPECTS OF THE PRACTICE	APPROACHES
Launching the discussion	• Framing the text and identifying a focal point for the discussion • Asking a question or making a statement to prime student thinking about the focal point in relation to the text • Making sure everyone understands the goal(s) • Reminding students of or establishing norms for the discussion
Creating opportunities for student talk	• Posing open-ended questions that support the overall point of focus of the discussion • Posing alternative/oppositional ideas for inquiry • Asking for clarification, expansion, or extension of an idea • Asking students to make connections

ASPECTS OF THE PRACTICE	APPROACHES
Coordinating student participation	• Encouraging and supporting participation from multiple students • Focusing attention on ideas being presented • Discerning particularly rich or distracting comments and helping the class to move the conversation toward the goal
Taking up student ideas	• Supporting student contributions through feedback or redirection • Repeating or rephrasing student contributions for the entire class to consider, in order to move the discussion in a productive direction, remediate important misconceptions, or probe interesting ideas • Adding academic language to a student contribution
Making contributions during the discussion	• At intervals, summarizing the big ideas presented and pushing the talk forward • Giving clarifying explanations when necessary • Making connections between important ideas that have been offered • Making connections between what is being said and the text under discussion • Redirecting the conversation if student contributions are moving away from the goals by making direct contributions or sidelining distracting ideas • Making judgments about when to participate and when not to, ensuring that one's own contributions do not prevent students from participating productively
Bringing the discussion to a close	• Acknowledging participation and work • Facilitating a synopsis in relation to the stated goal/purpose

Science Specification
of Facilitating Discussion

- **Definition/description of facilitating science discussion**
  Goals for discussion differ based on whether the discussion is, for instance, focused on eliciting student ideas, making sense from materials, observations, or data, or constructing explanations. While the goals of the discussion influence the selection of different elements of practice used by the teacher and shape opportunities for students' participation, in all cases the teacher ensures that student ideas are central to the discussion. The teacher also invokes the normative rules of discourse specific to the goals of the discussion. The following decomposition of the practice is focused on the teacher facilitating whole-class sense-making discussions; this kind of discussion follows an episode where students have worked with materials, gathered observations, and/or examined data.

ASPECTS OF FACILITATING SCIENCE DISCUSSION

ASPECTS OF THE PRACTICE	REQUIRED TECHNIQUES OR SKILLS
Framing the discussion	• Make the purpose of the discussion explicit for the students • Further frame the discussion through some subset of the following: - Make explicit the expectations for who should be participating (whether individuals or a representative from a group) - Establish norms for acceptable forms of talk (common vernacular and/or scientific language) - Providing examples of constructive talk - Establishing stance toward the use of evidence for supporting claims

ASPECTS OF THE PRACTICE	REQUIRED TECHNIQUES OR SKILLS

Publicly representing data and/or student ideas	• Anticipate the type of representation that is most beneficial to supporting the intellectual development of students
	• Elicit elements of student thinking that eventually would appear in a public representation
	• Decide when, how, and by whom public representations (lists of hypotheses, data displays, models of phenomena) can be modified in response to students' input
	• Make strategic decisions, based on assessment, about:
	  - Ideas that will be discussed
	  - How and what ideas are represented

Facilitating the discussion	• Recognize the need for and enact particular facilitation moves, including but not limited to:
	  - Using students' ideas as resources to move the discussion forward
	  - Pressing students for clarification or elaboration
	  - Rephrasing or re-voicing students' contributions
	  - Redirecting off-focus comments
	  - Asking students to comment on one another's thinking
	  - Using wait time
	  - Asking students to speak with a partner before sharing with the class

Closing the discussion	• Close the discussion using facilitation moves; these could include:
	  - Asking students to sum up
	  - Asking students "How do we think our thinking has changed today?"
	  - Asking students "What are we still confused about?"
	  - Asking students "What hypotheses are still plausible?"

NOTES

CHAPTER 1

1. John Dewey, "The Relation of Theory to Practice in Education," in *John Dewey: The Middle Works, 1899-1924*, vol. 3, ed. Jo Ann Boydston (Carbondale: Southern Illinois University Press, 1977), 249–272.
2. Laura M. Desimone and D. Long, "Teacher Effects and the Achievement Gap: Do Teacher and Teaching Quality Influence the Achievement Gap Between Black and White and High- and Low-SES Students in the Early Grades?," *Teachers College Record* 112, no. 12 (2010): 3024–73; William Sanders and S. Horn, "Research Findings from the Tennessee Value-Added Assessment System (TVAAS) Database: Implications for Educational Evaluation and Research," *Journal of Personnel Evaluation in Education* 12, no. 3 (1998): 247–56.
3. Pam Grossman and Morva McDonald, "Back to the Future: Directions for Research in Teaching and Teacher Education," *American Educational Research Journal* 45, no. 1 (March 1, 2008): 184–205, doi:10.3102/0002831207312906.
4. Pam Grossman, Karen Hammerness, and Morva McDonald, "Redefining Teaching, Re-Imagining Teacher Education," *Teachers and Teaching: Theory and Practice* 15, no. 2 (2009): 273–89; Ken Zeichner, "The Turn Once Again Toward Practice-Based Teacher Education," *Journal of Teacher Education* 63, no. 5 (November 1, 2012): 376–82, doi:10.1177/0022487112445789.
5. Deborah Ball and Francesca Forzani, "The Work of Teaching and the Challenge for Teacher Education," *Journal of Teacher Education* 60, no. 5 (November 1, 2009): 497–511, doi:10.1177/0022487109348479; Grossman, Hammerness, and McDonald, "Redefining Teaching, Re-Imagining Teacher Education"; Magdalene Lampert, "Learning Teaching In, From, and For Practice: What Do We Mean?," *Journal of Teacher Education* 61, no. 1–2 (2010): 21–34; Zeichner, "The Turn Once Again Toward Practice-Based Teacher Education."
6. Florida Department of Education, *Domains: Knowledge base of the Florida performance measurement system* (Tallahassee, FL: Office of Teacher Education, 1983).
7. Richard Shavelson and Stern, "Research on Teachers' Pedagogical Thoughts, Judgments, Decisions, and Behavior," *Review of Educational Research* 51, no. 4, (1981); Lee S. Shulman, "Knowledge and Teaching: Foundations of the New Reform," *Harvard Education Review* no. 1, (1987): 1–23.

8. Judith H. Shulman (Editor), *Case Methods in Teacher Education* (New York, NY: Teachers College Press, 1992).

9. Mary Kennedy, "The Role of Preservice Teacher Education," in *Teaching as the Learning Profession: Handbook of Teaching and Policy*, ed. Linda Darling-Hammond and Gary Sykes (San Francisco, CA: Jossey Bass, 1999), 54–86.

10. Grossman and McDonald, "Back to the Future"; Ball and Forzani, "The Work of Teaching and the Challenge for Teacher Education."

11. Grossman, Hammerness, and McDonald, "Redefining Teaching, Re-Imagining Teacher Education."

12. Morva McDonald, Elham Kazemi, and Sarah Schneider Kavanagh, "Core Practices and Pedagogies of Teacher Education: A Call for a Common Language and Collective Activity," *Journal of Teacher Education*, July 5, 2013, doi:10.1177/0022487113493807.

13. Pam Grossman, Karen Hammerness, and Morva McDonald, "Redefining Teaching, Re-Imagining Teacher Education," *Teachers and Teaching: Theory and Practice* 15, no. 2 (2009): 277.

14. Ball and Forzani, "The Work of Teaching and the Challenge for Teacher Education"; Deborah Ball and Francesca Forzani, "Building a Common Core for Learning to Teach, and Connecting Professional Learning to Practice," *American Educator* 35, no. 2 (2011): 17–21, 38–39.

15. Megan Loef Franke, Elham Kazemi, and D. Battey, "Understanding Teaching and Classroom Practice in Mathematics," in *Second Handbook of Research on Mathematics Teaching and Learning* (New York: Macmillian, 2007).

16. Bradley Fogo, "Core Practices for Teaching History: The Results of a Delphi Panel Survey," *Theory and Research in Social Education* 42, no. 2 (2014): 151–96; Matthew Kloser, "Identifying a Core Set of Science Teaching Practices: A Delphi Expert Panel Approach," *Journal of Research in Science Teaching* 51, no. 9 (November 1, 2014): 1185–1217, doi:10.1002/tea.21171.

17. Pam Grossman et al., "Teaching Practice: A Cross-Professional Perspective," *Teachers College Record* 111, no. 9 (2009): 2055–2100.

18. Pam Grossman et al., "Measure for Measure: The Relationship between Measures of Instructional Practice in Middle School English Language Arts and Teachers' Value-Added Scores," *American Journal of Education* 119, no. 3 (May 2013): 445–470.

19. Fogo, "Core Practices for Teaching History" and Kloser, "Identifying a Core Set of Science Teaching Practices."

20. Mark Windschitl et al., "Proposing a Core Set of Instructional Practices and Tools for Teachers of Science," *Science Education* 96, no. 5 (September 1, 2012): 878–903, doi:10.1002/sce.21027.

21. Abby Reisman et al., "Facilitating Whole-Class Discussions in History: A Framework for Preparing Teacher Candidates," *Journal of Teacher Education*, June 6, 2017, doi:10.1177/0022487117707463; Elizabeth Dutro and Ashey Cartun, "Cut to the Core Practices: Toward Visceral Disruptions of Binaries in PRACTICE-Based Teacher Education," *Teaching and Teacher Education* 58 (2016): 119–28; Chandra L. Alston et al., "Does a Discussion by Any Other Name Sound the Same? Teaching Discussion in Three ELA Methods Courses," *Journal of Teacher Education*, July 5, 2017, doi:10.1177/0022487117715227; Elizabeth A. Davis et al., "Teaching the Practice of Leading Sense-Making Discussions in Science: Science Teacher Educators Using Rehearsals," *Journal of Science Teacher Education*, 2017, doi:10.1080/1046560X.2017.1302729.

22. Grossman et al., "Teaching Practice: A Cross-Professional Perspective."

23. John Dewey, "The Relation of Theory to Practice in Education"; Sharon Feiman-Nemster and Margaret Buchmann, "Pitfalls of Experience in Teacher Education," *Teachers College Record* 87, no. 1 (1985): 53–65.

24. Grossman et al., "Teaching Practice: A Cross-Professional Perspective."

25. Charles Goodwin, "Professional Vision," *American Anthropologist* 96, no. 3 (September 1, 1994): 606–33, doi:10.1525/aa.1994.96.3.02a00100.

26. K. Anders Ericsson, "Attaining Excellence Through Deliberate Practice: Insights from the Study of Expert Performance," in *Teaching and Learning*, ed. Charles Desforges and Richard Fox (Blackwell Publishers Ltd, 2002), 4–37, http://onlinelibrary.wiley.com/doi/10.1002/9780470690048.ch1/summary.

27. Dan Lortie, *Schoolteacher: A Sociological Study* (Chicago: The University of Chicago Press, 1975).

CHAPTER 2

1. Pam Grossman et al., "Teaching Practice: A Cross-Professional Perspective," *Teachers College Record* 111, no. 9 (2009): 2055–2100.

2. Grossman et al., "Teaching Practice."

3. Morva McDonald, Elham Kazemi, and Sarah Schneider Kavanagh, "Core Practices and Pedagogies of Teacher Education: A Call for a Common Language and Collective Activity," *Journal of Teacher Education* 64, no. 5 (2013): 378–386; McDonald et al., "Teacher Education Pedagogy: Developing Core Practices across the Content Areas" (paper presented at the annual meeting of the American Association of Colleges for Teacher Education, Orlando, FL, February 2013).

4. Magdalene Lampert and Filippo Graziani, "Instructional Activities as a Tool for Teachers' and Teacher Educators' Learning in and for Practice." *Elementary School Journal* (2009).

5. Jeron Ashford Frame, *Yesterday I Had the Blues*, (Ten Speed Press, 2008).

6. "Interactive Read Aloud," Teacher Education by Design, http://tedd.org /activities/interactive-read-aloud.

7. Frame, *Yesterday I Had the Blues.*

8. Deborah Loewenberg Ball, Mark Hoover Thames, Geoffrey Phelps, "Content Knowledge for Teaching: What Makes it Special?", *Journal of Teacher Education* 59, no. 5 (2008): 389–407.

9. Kristine Schutz, Katie Danielson, and Julie Cohen, "Approximations in English Language Arts: Scaffolding a Shared Teaching Practice" (under review).

10. Abby Reisman, "Reading Like a Historian: A Document-Based History Curriculum Intervention in Urban High Schools," *Cognition and Instruction* 30, no. 1 (2012).

11. Deborah Loewenberg Ball, Mark Hoover Thames, Geoffrey Phelps, "Content Knowledge for Teaching: What Makes it Special?"

CHAPTER 3

1. Allan Collins, John Seely Brown, and Ann Holum, "Cognitive Apprenticeship: Making Thinking Visible," *American Educator* 15, no. 3 (1991); Gerald G. Duffy, Laura R. Roehler, and Beth Ann Herrmann, "Modeling Mental Process Helps Poor Readers Become Strategic Readers," *The Reading Teacher* 41 (1988); Annemarie Sullivan Palinscar and Deborah A. Brown, "Enhancing Instructional Time Through Attention to Metacognition," *Journal of Learning Disabilities* 20, no. 2 (1987).

2. Charles Goodwin, "Professional Vision," *American Anthropologist* 96 (1994): 606.

3. Catherine E. Snow and Gina Biancarosa, *Adolescent Literacy Development Among English Language Learners* (New York, NY: Carnegie Corporation, 2003); see also Annemarie Sullivan Palincsar et al., "Promoting Deep Understanding of Science in Students with Disabilities in Inclusion Classrooms," *Learning Disabilities Quarterly* 24, no. 1 (2001).

4. Pam Grossman et al., "Measure for Measure: The Relationship Between Measures of Instructional Practice in Middle School English Language Arts and Teachers' Value-Added Scores," *American Journal of Education* 119 (2013): 13–14.

5. Sarah Kate Selling, "Cultivating Learning Opportunities for Mathematical Practices in Urban Middle and High School Mathematics Classes" (unpublished doctoral dissertation, Stanford University, 2014).

6. Deborah Loewenberg Ball, Imani Masters Goffney, and Hyman Bass, "The Role of Mathematics Instruction in Building a Socially Just and Diverse Democracy," *The Mathematics Educator* 15, no. 1 (2005): 3.

7. Imani Masters Goffney, "Identifying, Measuring, and Defining Equitable Mathematics Instruction" (unpublished doctoral dissertation, University of Michigan, 2010).
8. Deborah Loewenberg Ball and Francesca M. Forzani, "The Work of Teaching and the Challenge of Teacher Education," *Journal of Teacher Education* 60, no. 5 (2009); Pam Grossman and Morva McDonald, "Back to the Future: Directions for Research in Teaching and Teacher Education," *American Educational Research Journal* 45 (2008).

CHAPTER 4

1. Pam Grossman et al., "Teaching Practice: A Cross-Professional Perspective," *Teachers College Record* 111, no. 9 (2009): 2055–2100.
2. Grossman et al., "Teaching Practice."
3. Fred Janssen, Pam Grossman, and Hanna Westbroek, "Facilitating Decomposition and Recomposition in Practice-Based Teacher Education: The Power of Modularity," *Teaching and Teacher Education* 51 (2016): 137–146.
4. Magdalene Lampert and Filippo Graziani, "Instructional Activities as a Tool for Teachers' and Teacher Educators' Learning In and For Practice," *Elementary School Journal* 109, no. 5 (2009): 491–509.
5. Kristine M. Schutz, Katie A. Danielson, and Julie J. Cohen, "Approximation in English Language Arts: Scaffolding a Shared Teaching Practice," *Teaching and Teacher Education* (under review).
6. Mary Kennedy, "The Role of Preservice Teacher Education," in *Teaching as the Learning Profession: Handbook of Policy and Practice*, eds. Linda Darling-Hammond and Gary Sykes (San Francisco: Jossey Bass, 1999), 54–85.
7. Chandra Alston et al., "Does a Discussion by Any Other Name Sound the Same? Teaching Discussion in Three ELA Methods Courses," *Journal of Teacher Education* (2017).
8. Linda Kucan and Annemarie S. Palincsar, *Comprehension Instruction Through Text-Based Discussion* (Newark, DE: International Reading Association, 2013).
9. Sarah Schneider Kavanagh, "Practicing Social Justice: Towards a Practice-Based Approach to Learning to Teach for Social Justice," in *Reflective Theories in Teacher Education Practice: Process, Impact, and Enactment*, eds. Robyn Brandenburg et al. (Singapore: Springer, 2017), 161–175.
10. Miriam Schiffer, *Stella Brings the Family* (San Francisco: Chronicle Books, 2015).
11. Grossman et al., "Teaching Practice."
12. Nell K. Duke and Kristine M. Schutz, "Prompts for When a Child is Having Difficulty Reading a Word" (unpublished document, University of Michigan, 2017).

CHAPTER 5

1. Elizabeth Davis et al., "Teaching the Practice of Leading Sensemaking Discussions in Science: Science Teacher Educators Using Rehearsals," *Journal of Science Teacher Education* 28 (2017): 275–293; Magdalene Lampert et al., "Keeping It Complex: Using Rehearsals to Support Novice Teacher Learning of Ambitious Teaching," *Journal of Teacher Education* 64 (2013): 226–243.
2. Davis et al., "Teaching the Practice of Leading Sensemaking Discussions"; Lampert et al., "Keeping it complex."
3. Lampert et al., "Keeping it complex."
4. Davis et al., "Teaching the Practice of Leading Sensemaking Discussions."
5. D.C. Lortie, *Schoolteacher: A Sociological Study* (Chicago: University of Chicago Press, 1975).

CHAPTER 6

1. Elizabeth A. Davis and Timothy Boerst, "Designing Elementary Teacher Education to Prepare Well-Started Beginners" (working paper, TeachingWorks, University of Michigan School of Education, Ann Arbor, 2014).
2. Magdalene Lampert et al., "Keeping It Complex: Using Rehearsals to Support Novice Teacher Learning of Ambitious Teaching," *Journal of Teacher Education* 64, no. 3 (2013): 226–243.
3. Morva McDonald, Elham Kazemi, and Sarah Schneider Kavanagh, "Core Practices and Pedagogies of Teacher Education: A Call for a Common Language and Collective Activity," *Journal of Teacher Education* 64, no. 5 (2013): 378–386.
4. Kara J. Jackson et al., "Launching Complex Tasks," *Mathematics Teaching in the Middle School* 18, no. 1 (2012): 24–29; Margaret S. Smith et al., "Orchestrating Discussions," *Mathematics Teaching in the Middle School* 14, no. 9 (2009): 548–556.
5. https://www.edtpa.com/
6. https://www.k-12leadership.org/content/service/5-dimensions-of-teaching-and-learning
7. Elizabeth Dutro and Ashley Cartun, "Cut to the Core Practices: Toward Visceral Disruptions of Binaries in PRACTICE-Based Teacher Education," *Teaching and Teacher Education* 58 (2016): 119–128.
8. Victoria Trinder, "A Decolonizing Teacher Preparation Framework" (paper presented at the UIC College of Education Research Day, Chicago, October 3, 2014).
9. Catherine E. Snow and Anne Polselli Sweet, "Reading for Comprehension," in *Rethinking Reading Comprehension,* eds. Anne Polselli Sweet and Catherine E. Snow (New York: Guilford Press, 2003), 1–11.

10. McDonald, Kazemi, and Schneider Kavanagh, "Core Practices and Pedagogies of Teacher Education."

11. Victoria Purcell-Gates, *Other People's Words: The Cycle of Low Literacy* (Boston: Harvard Educational Press, 1995).

12. Django Paris and H. Samy Alim, eds. *Culturally Sustaining Pedagogies: Teaching and Learning for Justice in a Changing World* (Teachers College Press, 2017).

13. Michael Hall, *Red: A Crayon's Story* (New York: Greenwillow Books, 2015).

14. Kristine uses this text again in the second-semester literacy course as candidates begin to explore concepts for critical conversations about texts such as representation, gender, race, and class. Candidates return to *Red* by Michael Hall and identify concepts that could be addressed through the text.

15. Jacqueline Woodson, *The Other Side* (New York: G.P. Putnam's Sons Books for Young Readers, 2001).

16. Jeron Ashford Frame, *Yesterday I Had the Blues* (Berkeley: Tricycle Press, 2008).

17. Mary Ann Rodman, *My Best Friend* (New York: Puffin, 2007).

18. Kristine M. Schutz, Emily Rainey, and Stefanie Iwashyna, "Decomposing and Describing Modeling as a Core Practice in Elementary Literacy" (paper presented at the Annual Meeting of the Literacy Research Association, Marco Island, Florida, December 2014).

19. "Core Practice Consortium," http://corepracticeconsortium.com.

CHAPTER 7

1. Abby Reisman, "Entering the Historical Problem Space: Whole-Class, Text-Based Discussion in History Class," *Teachers College Record* 117, no. 2 (2015): 1–44.

2. Abby Reisman, Sarah Kavanagh, Chauncey Monte-Sano, Brad Fogo, Sarah McGrew, Peter Cipparone, and Elizabeth Simmons, "Facilitating Whole-Class Discussions in History: A Framework for Preparing Teacher Candidates," *Journal of Teacher Education* (2017), doi: 10.1177/0022487117707463.

3. Miriam Gamoran Sherin and Elizabeth van Es, "Using Video to Support Teachers' Ability to Notice Classroom Interactions," *Journal of Technology and Teacher Education* 13, no. 3 (2005): 475–491; Miriam Gamoran Sherin and Elizabeth van Es, "Mathematics Teachers' 'Learning to Notice' in the Context of a Video Club," *Teaching and Teacher Education* 24, no. 2 (2008): 244–276.

4. Morva McDonald, Elham Kazemi, and Sarah Schneider Kavanagh, "Core Practices and Pedagogies of Teacher Education" *Journal of Teacher Education* 64, no. 5 (2013): 378–386.

5. Charles Goodwin, "Professional Vision," *American Anthropologist* 96, no. 3 (1994): 606–633; Pamela Grossman, et al. "Teaching Practice: A Cross-Professional Perspective," *Teachers College Record* 11, no. 9 (2009): 2055–2100;

Reed Stevens and Rogers Hall, "Disciplined Perception: Learning to See in Technoscience," *Talking Mathematics in School: Studies of Teaching and Learning* (1998): 107–149.

6. Lynsey Gibbons, Elham Kazemi, and Rebecca Lewis, "Developing Collective Capacity to Improve Mathematics Instruction: Coaching as a Lever for School-Wide Improvement," *Journal of Mathematical Behavior.* (2017).

7. Clea Fernandez, "Learning from Japanese Approaches to Professional Development: The Case of Lesson Study," *Journal of Teacher Education* 53, no. 5 (2002): 393–405.

8. Lynsey Gibbons, Elham Kazemi, Allison Hintz, and Elizabeth Hartmann, "Teacher Time Out: Educators Learning Together In and Through Practice," *Journal of Mathematics Educational Leadership* (in press).

APPENDIX

1. Reprinted from: TeachingWorks, "High-Leverage Practices," Teachingworks .org. http://www.teachingworks.org/work-of-teaching/high-leverage-practices.

2. Reprinted from: Sarah Schneider Kavanagh, Emily Shahan, and Deb Morrison, "Core Practices of Teaching: A Primer," TEDD.org. http://coetedd.wpengine .netdna-cdn.com/wp-content/uploads/2017/09/core_practice_primer.pdf.

3. Reprinted from: http://platorubric.stanford.edu/Elements.html#pur.

4. Reprinted from: Matthew Kloser, "Identifying a Core Set of Science Teaching Practices: A Delphi Expert Panel Approach," *Journal of Research in Science Teaching,* 51 (2014): 1185–1217.

5. Reprinted from: Bradley Fogo, "Core Practices for Teaching History: The Results of a Delphi Panel Survey," *Theory and Research in Social Education,* 42:2 (2014): 151–196.

ACKNOWLEDGMENTS

Hannah Arendt once claimed that "for excellence, the presence of others is always required." In the case of the work that led to this book, the presence of others was not only a necessity but a constant source of joy and learning. We would like to acknowledge all members of the Core Practice Consortium, past, present, and future, who have contributed so much to the ideas in this book and to the continuous improvement of teacher education: Chandra Alston, Deborah Ball, Andrea Bien, Janet Carlson, Ashley Cartun, Peter Cipparone, Julie Cohen, Katie Danielson, Betsy Davis, Elizabeth Dutro, Brad Fogo, Francesca Forzani, Megan Franke, Hala Ghousseini, Pam Grossman, Elizabeth Hartmann, Lightning Jay, Sarah Schneider Kavanagh, Elham Kazemi, Megan Kelley-Petersen, Sara Kersey, Matt Kloser, Magdalene Lampert, Morva McDonald, Sarah McGrew, Chauncey Monte-Sano, Jamie O'Keefe, Christoper Pupik Dean, Abby Reisman, Kristine Schutz, Emily Shahan, Meghan Shaughnessy, Elizabeth Simmons, Jessica Thompson, Andrea Wells, and Mark Windschitl.

We would also like to thank our colleagues, thought partners, and students who worked with us and contributed to our thinking and practice over the past decade as we experimented with these ideas: Merrie Blunk, Tim Boerst, Lindsay Brown, Raedell Cannie, Brad Cawn, Susanna Farmer, Nicole Garcia, Mary Hauser, Diana Hess, Erika Moore Johnson, Debi Khasnabis, Linda Kucan, Emily Machado, Lindsey Mann, Mike Metz, Jason Moore, Annemarie Palincsar, Cathy Reischl, Janine Remillard, Mike Rose, Clare Donovan Scane, Melissa Scheve, Lorien Chambers Schuldt, Sarah Scott Frank, Sarah Kate Selling, Vicki Trinder, Sheila Valencia, and Becca Woodard. We would also like to thank Marilyn Baffoe-Bonnie for her assistance in preparing the final manuscript.

We are indebted to the Bill and Melinda Gates Foundation for their generous support of the work of the Core Practice Consortium, and to Michelle Riojas, who was a terrific thought partner in her role as program officer. We would also like to gratefully acknowledge the Spencer Foundation for its support of this work.

We would also like to acknowledge our editor, Caroline Chauncey, who was the best cheerleader anyone could hope for as we brought this book to fruition.

Finally, we would like to acknowledge all of the teacher candidates with whom we have worked. You are the future of our profession, and the students you teach, in turn, are our best hope for the future.

ABOUT THE EDITOR

PAM GROSSMAN is the Dean of the Graduate School of Education and the George and Diane Weiss Professor of Education at the University of Pennsylvania. Prior to her position at Penn, Dr. Grossman was the Nomellini-Olivier Professor of Education at the Stanford University School of Education, where she founded and led the Center to Support Excellence in Teaching. Dr. Grossman's research focuses on the preparation of teachers and other professionals and on teaching quality. Her most recent work focuses on practice-based teacher education and the role of core practices of teaching in teacher preparation and professional development. She was elected to the National Academy of Education in 2009 and currently sits on the Academy's Board of Directors. She is Chair of the Spencer Foundation Board of Directors and a member of the Board of the Carnegie Foundation for the Advancement of Teaching. She was elected to the American Association of Arts and Sciences in 2017.

ABOUT THE CONTRIBUTORS

CHANDRA L. ALSTON is an assistant professor in Educational Studies and lead faculty in English Language Arts for Secondary Teacher Education at the University of Michigan School of Education. She also works closely with the Joint PhD Program in English and Education. Alston investigates the influence of various levers on the goal of providing equitable and accessible instruction for marginalized and minoritized youth, particularly literacy instruction in secondary schools. This work has included investigations of value-added modeling, writing instruction, teacher education pedagogies, and policy reforms such as the Common Core State Standards. She received her PhD in curriculum and teacher education from Stanford University.

ANDREA BIEN is a clinical assistant professor in Elementary Education at Boston University. Her research interests include elementary literacy teaching and learning, practice-based teacher education, and job-embedded teacher professional learning. At BU, Andrea teaches literacy methods courses for undergraduate and graduate preservice teacher candidates on-site at a Boston Public Schools elementary school. Andrea's work with teachers and students in the Boston Public Schools also includes coaching BU candidates in their pre-practicum and practicum field experiences, supporting BU candidates' cooperating teachers through professional learning experiences designed to focus on mentorship practice, and facilitating job-embedded learning labs focusing on discussion in literacy with K–8 teachers. Prior to her position at BU, Andrea was a postdoc at the University of Washington, where she was a literacy methods instructor and coach in UW's Seattle Teacher Residency program. Andrea earned her doctorate in Literacy Curriculum & Instruction from the University of Colorado Boulder.

JANET CARLSON is an associate professor (research) at the Stanford Graduate School of Education and executive director of the Center to Support Excellence in Teaching. Dr. Carlson's research interests include the impact of educative curriculum materials and transformative professional development on science teaching and learning. She began her career as a middle and high school science teacher and has spent the last twenty years working in science education developing curriculum, leading professional development, and conducting research. Dr. Carlson received her PhD in Instruction and Curriculum (science education) from the University of Colorado.

ASHLEY CARTUN is the director of Elementary Teacher Education Field Experiences and part of the Elementary Education teaching faculty at the University of Colorado Boulder. Her current research interests include critical literacy, teacher education, affect theory, reading and writing education, and young adult and children's literature. Ashley's current research focuses on teacher education, writing in the elementary grades, and pedagogies of affect and emotion in relation to knowledge, power, and literacies.

KATIE A. DANIELSON is a postdoctoral fellow in the department of Teaching and Learning at New York University's Steinhardt School of Culture, Education, and Human Development. Her research focuses on teaching and teacher education in literacy. She is also interested in the role of vocabulary, discourse, and strategy instruction to support children in learning to comprehend and compose complex texts. Katie earned her doctorate at the University of Washington, where she worked on teacher education program design and taught elementary literacy methods. She is a member of the English/Language Arts team in the Core Practice Consortium.

ELIZABETH A. (BETSY) DAVIS is a science educator and teacher educator at the University of Michigan whose research interests include teacher and student learning. She is especially interested in beginning and experienced elementary teachers, teachers learning to engage in ambitious science teaching, and the roles of curriculum materials and teacher education in promoting teacher learning. Davis received her doctorate from the University of California at Berkeley in 1998, and received the Presidential Early Career Award for Scientists and Engineers at the White House in 2002 and the Jan Hawkins Early Career Award in 2004. She was inducted into Phi Kappa Phi in 2015. Davis has published in journals such as *Science Education, Journal of Research in Science Teaching, Teaching and Teacher Education, Curriculum Inquiry*, and *Educational Researcher*.

CHRISTOPHER G. PUPIK DEAN is the director of the Independent School Teaching Residency program and a Senior Fellow at the University of Pennsylvania's Graduate School of Education. Dr. Pupik Dean taught high school science in North Carolina for five years before beginning his graduate studies. Dr. Pupik Dean's research focuses on teacher education, project-based learning, and the impact of humanities education on civic development.

BRAD FOGO is an assistant professor of teacher education in the Graduate College of Education at San Francisco State University. His research focuses on instructional practice, curriculum development, and teacher learning in history–social studies education.

MEGAN FRANKE is a professor of Education at the University of California, Los Angeles. Dr. Franke's research focuses on understanding and supporting teacher learning for both preservice and in-service teachers. She designs, prepares, and studies the preparation of early childhood to sixth grade mathematics teachers.

HALA GHOUSSEINI is an associate professor in the Department of Curriculum and Instruction at the University of Wisconsin-Madison. Her research focuses on understanding the nature of teacher learning and practice-based designs of professional education. She has several years of experience both as a teacher and as a professional developer of teachers.

LIGHTNING PETER JAY is a doctoral student in the Teaching, Learning, and Teacher Education program at the University of Pennsylvania, where he also teaches in the Teacher Education Program. Before attending Penn, Lightning taught history to middle and high school students in Minneapolis, Minn., and Brooklyn, N.Y.

SARAH SCHNEIDER KAVANAGH is a research assistant professor of teacher education in the Graduate School of Education at the University of Pennsylvania. Her work investigates the relationship between teacher education pedagogy and the instructional practice of novice teachers. She comes to her current position from Stanford University's Center to Support Excellence in Teaching, where she was a postdoctoral scholar, and from a position as a research scientist at the University of Washington's College of Education, where she started the Mentor Labs Project, a research and development initiative focused on transforming the practice of teacher mentoring in K–12 schools. Additionally, she is the founding director of Teacher Education by Design (TEDD.org), an open-source curricular library of practice-based tools for teacher education. She began her career in education as a classroom teacher, first in the Bay area and then in the Baltimore area.

ELHAM KAZEMI is the Geda and Phil Condit Professor of Mathematics Education at the University of Washington. She is currently involved in several efforts to redesign teacher preparation and professional development for and with elementary teachers. The aim is to develop instructional practices that advance student learning and lead to positive engagement with mathematics, especially in schools serving historically marginalized populations. She is studying how strong professional communities develop and the role that principals and coaches play in organizing schools for meaningful teacher and student learning. Her work with teachers is informed by equity-oriented research on organizational learning, children's mathematical thinking, and classroom discourse.

MEGAN KELLEY-PETERSEN is the director of the University-Accelerated Certification for Teachers Program at the University of Washington. Dr. Kelley-Petersen earned her PhD at the University of Washington in Curriculum and Instruction, with a focus in Elementary Mathematics. Before her work at UW, she was an elementary school teacher and elementary math coach in the Seattle Public School District, in addition to facilitating professional development across the country. Her research focuses on teacher education and preparation, and on teaching and learning in elementary mathematics.

MATTHEW KLOSER is the founding director of the Center for STEM Education and a faculty member and Fellow of the Institute for Educational Initiatives at the University of Notre Dame. Dr. Kloser's research focuses on issues of teaching, learning, and assessment in science classrooms with a special focus on biology education. His research includes experimental studies that identify affordances and constraints of learning biology from different text types, mixed-method studies focused on assessment implications for student outcomes, and the relationship between core instructional practices and student outcomes. Dr. Kloser received his M.Ed. through the Alliance for Catholic Education program at the University of Notre Dame and taught high school physics and math for five years prior to earning his M.S. in biology and Ph.D. in science education from Stanford University.

SARAH MCGREW is a doctoral candidate in Curriculum and Teacher Education at Stanford University, where she has taught in the Stanford Teacher Education Program. Before starting her doctoral work, she was a world history teacher in Washington, D.C.

CHAUNCEY MONTE-SANO is an associate professor of Educational Studies at the University of Michigan. A former high school history teacher and National Board Certified teacher, she prepares novice teachers for the social studies classroom and works with veteran social studies teachers through a variety of professional development programs. Her research examines how students learn to reason with evidence as they write in history and social sciences, and how their teachers learn to teach such disciplinary thinking. She has won research grants from the Library of Congress, Institute of Education Sciences, the Spencer Foundation, and the Braitmayer Foundation, as well as awards from the National Council for the Social Studies, the American Historical Association, and Division K of the American Educational Research Association.

ABBY REISMAN is an assistant professor of Teacher Education at the University of Pennsylvania's Graduate School of Education. Her research focuses on how to engage adolescents in text-based historical inquiry. In addition to curriculum design, her interests include the design of preservice teacher education and professional development around core instructional practices. She received her Ph.D. from Stanford University, where she directed the "Reading Like a Historian" Project in San Francisco, the first extended history curriculum intervention in urban high schools. She began her career in education as a classroom teacher in a small, progressive high school in New York City.

MELISSA A. SCHEVE, a National Board Certified teacher and a finalist for Massachusetts teacher of the year, is the project director for Stanford University's Hollyhock Fellowship Program, which supports early-career educators who teach in historically underserved communities in developing their practice and extending their time in the classroom. Before Hollyhock, Mrs. Scheve spent two decades teaching in high schools across the country—most recently at a public charter school in New Haven, Conn., where she served as a mentor teacher and department chair.

KRISTINE M. SCHUTZ is an assistant professor in Curriculum and Instruction at the University of Illinois at Chicago. Her research interests include elementary literacy instruction, practice-based teacher education, and design settings for classroom-situated teacher learning. At UIC, she teaches literacy methods courses in the urban education program and courses in perspectives on reading, literacy leadership, and teacher education at the graduate level. Prior to her position at UIC, she was the lead literacy research and design specialist at TeachingWorks. Kristine earned her doctorate in Literacy, Language, and Culture from the University of Michigan where she contributed to the redesign of the teacher education program and taught a school-embedded literacy methods course.

MEGHAN SHAUGHNESSY is a teacher educator and researcher at the University of Michigan School of Education. Her research focuses on the study and improvement of mathematics instruction, specifically practice-intensive approaches to the professional training of teachers, and assessment of developing skills with teaching practices. She received a PhD in Mathematics Education from the University of California, Berkeley.

ANDREA WELLS is a co-director of the Apprenticeship Program and Professional Development facilitator for the Next Generation Science Exemplar (NGSX) project. She is also a doctoral student at Boston University, where her adviser is Dr. Eve Manz. Prior to this, Andrea was a clinical teacher educator with Boston Teacher Residency for six years, where she taught the secondary science methods course and coached and supervised all science residents in their residency placements in the Boston Public Schools. She collaborated in the development of clinical teacher education pedagogies that focused on residents learning in and from their classroom practice by connecting their teaching directly with student learning. In her work with the residents, she focused particularly on the core practice of content-focused whole-class discussion, and specifically on teaching residents to use productive talk to support all students to build a deep understanding of science concepts. Her work as a teacher educator is informed by ten years of teaching secondary science in Chicago and the area. Andrea earned her M.Ed. from the Harvard Graduate School of Education in Mind, Brain, and Education.

INDEX